Basic Arabic

Grade 1 & 2

PART 1

Learning Arabic is fun.

Written and compiled
by
Marius du Plooy

ISBN-13: 978-1517747770

ISBN-10: 1517747775

Content

Introduction

Basic Arabic Writing manual is the first edition in this series to teach children who take Arabic as a second language. Great affort has been taken in this book to make learning an interesting, yet informative way of learning. Each lesson inlcudes engaging exercises to stimulate active participation from the learner.

Each lesson contains pratical writing exercises with the pronounciation for each letter of the Arabic letter being provided. The lessons give the student the opportunity to develop the necessary writing skills required to write the Arabic script.

Parents play an important role in the early stages of a child's education. One of the obstacles in teaching Arabic is that the parents were unable to help their child since they did not speak Arabic. At this point the help of modern technology is indispensable. Each lesson contains Youtube videos to guide the parent in helping her or his child at home. The videos also function as a revision for the learner. They have been designed to make the learning experience for the student a fun activity. Many of the characters in the videos have been drawn by children of TAWAM INTERNATIONAL SCHOOL in Buraimi, Oman.

In order to access the Youtube vidoes follow these instructions:
1. Go to www.youtube.com.
2. Type in marios arabic at the search place.
3. Click on the channel which has super mario as an icon.
4. Select playlists from the channel and choose speaking lessons to start.

This language course is focussed on everyday language usage in the Arab culture. Familiar themes and
topics form an intergal part of methodology of this course. The main objective through this firts series is
that your child will improve his/her language ability and experience it as a joyful and fun way of learning
a new language.

Marius du Plooy

The Arabic Alphabet

Arabic	Name	Pronounciation
ا	alif	Like the "a" in apple
ب	baa	Like the "b" in boy
ت	taa	Like the "t" in table
ث	thaa	Like the "th" in think
ج	jiim	Like the "j" in measure
ح	Ha	Like the "H" when you are cleaning your glasses
خ	kha	Like the "kha" in Bach
د	daal	Like the "d" in door
ذ	dhaal	Like the "th" in those
ر	ra	Like the "r" in round
ز	za	Like the "z" in zebra
س	siin	Like the "s" in snake

The Arabic Alphabet

Arabic	Name	Pronounciation
ش	shiin	Like the "sh" in sheep
ص	Saad	A deep "s" sound. Keep your tongue on the lower teeth
ض	Daad	A deep "d" sound. Keep your tongue on the lower teeth
ط	Ta	A deep "t" sound. Keep your tongue on the lower teeth
ظ	Twa	Like the "tha" in that
ع	Ayn	An "a" – sound but pronounced from the throat
غ	ghayn	Like the sound when you gargle
ف	fa	Like the "f" in floor
ق	qaaf	A "k" – sound but pronounced from the throat
ك	kaaf	Like the "k" in keeper
ل	laam	Like the "l" in long
م	miim	Like the "m" more

The Arabic Alphabet

Arabic	Name	Pronounciation
ن	nun	Like the "n" in no
هـ	he	Like the "h" in hard
و	waw	Like the "w" in winner or Like the "oo" in soon
ي	ya	Like the "y" in yes or Like the "ee" in seen
ء	hamza	A stop-sound like in oh-oh

Lesson 1

Section A: Writing

١	⋮	ا
ب	ب	ب
ت	ت	ت
ث	ث	ث
ج	ج	ج
ح	ح	ح

The Arabic Alphabet

Name: Alif   **Pronunciation: 'a' like in b<u>a</u>t**

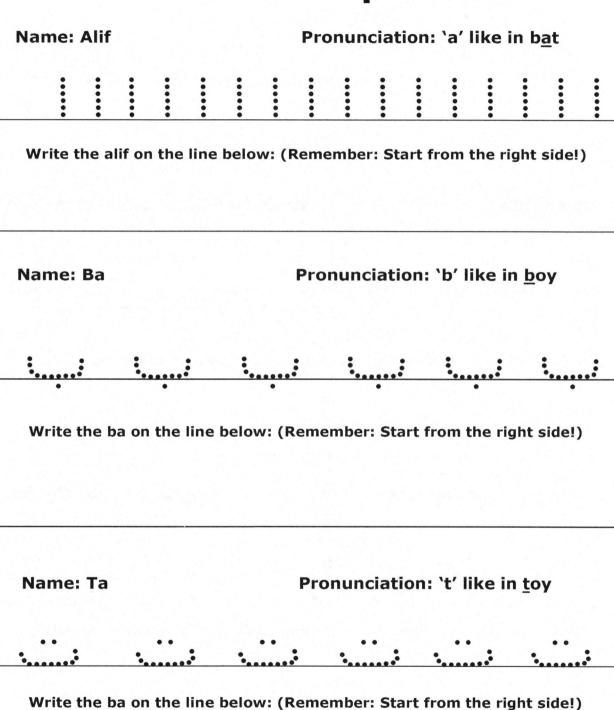

Write the alif on the line below: (Remember: Start from the right side!)

Name: Ba   **Pronunciation: 'b' like in <u>b</u>oy**

Write the ba on the line below: (Remember: Start from the right side!)

Name: Ta   **Pronunciation: 't' like in <u>t</u>oy**

Write the ba on the line below: (Remember: Start from the right side!)

Name: Tha   Pronunciation: 'th' like in <u>think</u>

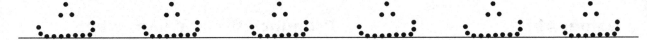

Write the tha on the line below: (Remember: Start from the right side!)

_____

Name: Jiim   Pronunciation: 'j' like in mea<u>s</u>ure

Write the jiim on the line below: (Remember: Start from the right side!)

_____

Name: Ha Pronunciation: 'H' like in you are cleaning your classes

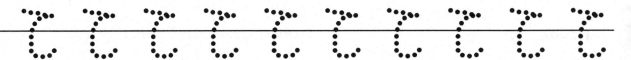

Write the Ha on the line below: (Remember: Start from the right side!)

_____

3

Exercise 1

a) Draw a ☐ around the alif.

b) Draw a △ around the ba.

c) Draw a ◯ around the ta.

d) Draw a ◇ around the tha.

e) Draw a ☆ around the jiim.

f) Draw a ⬡ around the Ha.

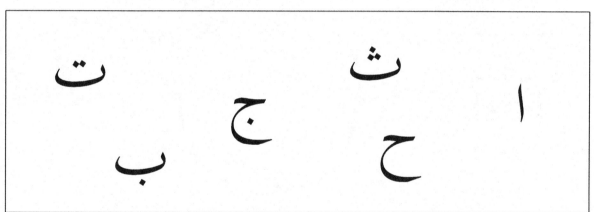

ت   ث

ج   ا

ب   ح

You Tube Videos:

Watch the youtube video below to see how we write and pronounce these letters.

2:56

Writing Arabic: The Alphabet
Part 1

Just type 'marios arabic'
at youtube search.

4

Exercise 2: Colouring

باب
baab

تفاحة
tufaaha

أرنب
arnab

ثَوب
thaub

جمل
jamal

Hosaan حصان

Writing practise

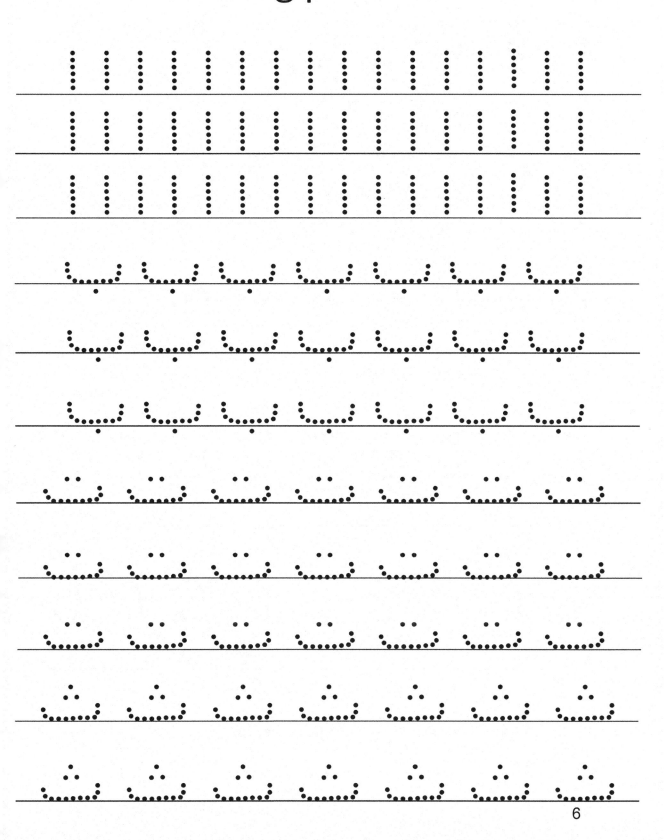

Writing practise

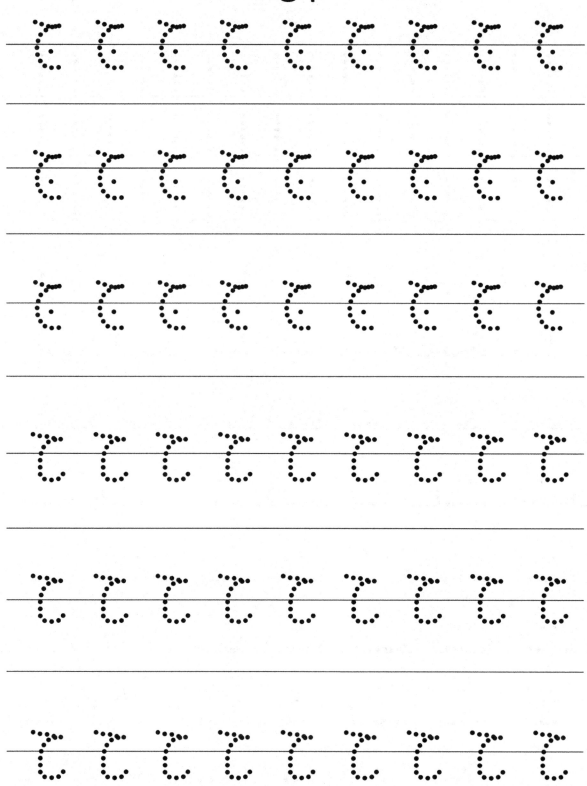

Section B: Conversation
Greetings

و عليكم السلام

Wa alekum assalaam

and peace on you

السلام عليكم

Assalaam alekum

Peace on you

الحمد الله بخير

ilhamdulilah bakheer

Praise God, well

كيف حالك

kayf Haalak?

How are you?

You Tube Video: Lesson 1 Greetings

Vocabulary

English	Transliteration	Arabic
Rabbit	arnab	ارنب
door	baab	باب
apple	tufaaHa	تفاحة
robe	thaub	ثوب
camel	jamal	جمل
horse	HuSaan	حصان
peace	salaam	سلام
on you	alekum	عليكم
praise God	ilhamdulilah	الحمد الله
well, fine	bakheer	بخير

Assessment : Lesson 1

Listen to your teacher and mark the letter with a X which he/she pronounce.

| 1 | ا | ث | ح | ب | ج | ت |

| 2 | ت | ح | ا | ج | ب | ث |

| 3 | ج | ت | ح | ب | ا | ث |

| 4 | ث | ا | ج | ح | ب | ت |

| 5 | ج | ب | ث | ج | ت | ح |

| 6 | ح | ت | ث | ب | ج | ا |

| 7 | ث | ج | ا | ح | ت | ب |

| 8 | ت | ا | ب | ج | ح | ث |

Lesson 2
Section A: Writing

	ﺡ	ﺥ
	ﺩ	ﺩ
	ﺩ	ﻥ
	ﺭ	ﺭ
	ﺭ	ﺯ
	ﺱ	ﺱ

The Arabic Alphabet

Name: Kha   **Pronunciation: 'kh' like in ba<u>ch</u>**

ﺥ ﺥ ﺥ ﺥ ﺥ ﺥ ﺥ ﺥ ﺥ

Write the kha on the line below: (Remember: Start from the right side!)

Name: Daal   **Pronunciation: 'd' like in <u>d</u>oor**

ﺩ ﺩ ﺩ ﺩ ﺩ ﺩ ﺩ ﺩ ﺩ ﺩ

Write the daal on the line below: (Remember: Start from the right side!)

Name: dhaal   **Pronunciation: 'th' like in <u>th</u>ose**

ﺫ ﺫ ﺫ ﺫ ﺫ ﺫ ﺫ ﺫ ﺫ ﺫ ﺫ ﺫ

Write the dhaal on the line below: (Remember: Start from the right side!)

The Arabic Alphabet

Name: ra   **Pronunciation: 'r' like in round**

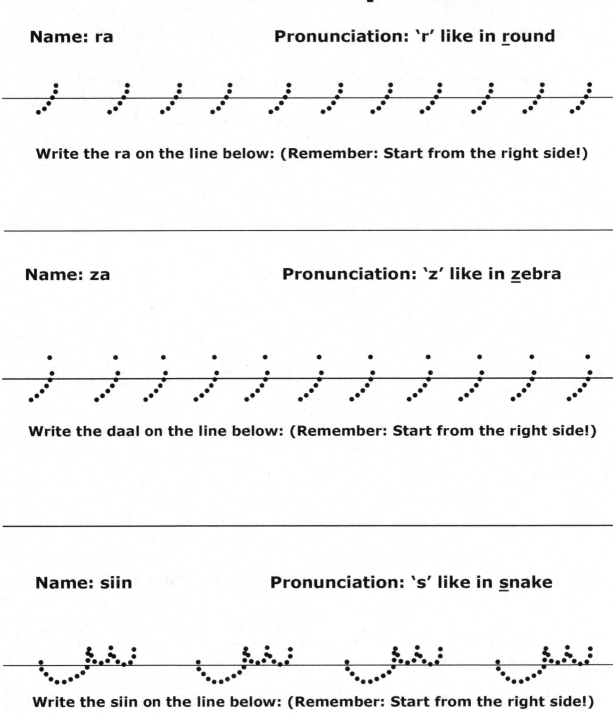

Write the ra on the line below: (Remember: Start from the right side!)

Name: za   **Pronunciation: 'z' like in zebra**

Write the daal on the line below: (Remember: Start from the right side!)

Name: siin   **Pronunciation: 's' like in snake**

Write the siin on the line below: (Remember: Start from the right side!)

Exercise 3

Connect the Arabic letter with it's name

ra

siin

kha

za

dhaal

daal

خ

د

ذ

ر

ز

س

You Tube Video:

Watch the youtube video below to see how we write and pronounce these letters.

2:56

Writing Arabic: The Alphabet
Part 1

Just type 'marios arabic'
at youtube search.

Exercise: Colouring

خْ

خُبْز

khubz

د

دجاج

dajaaj

ذهب

dhahab

gold

رجل

rajul

س

سمكة

samaka

ن

زرافة

zaraafa

Writing practise

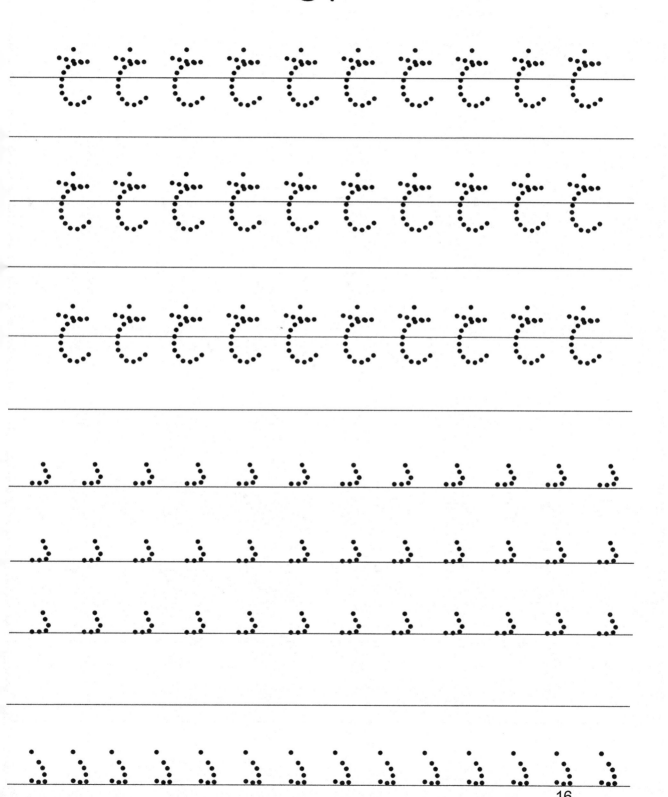

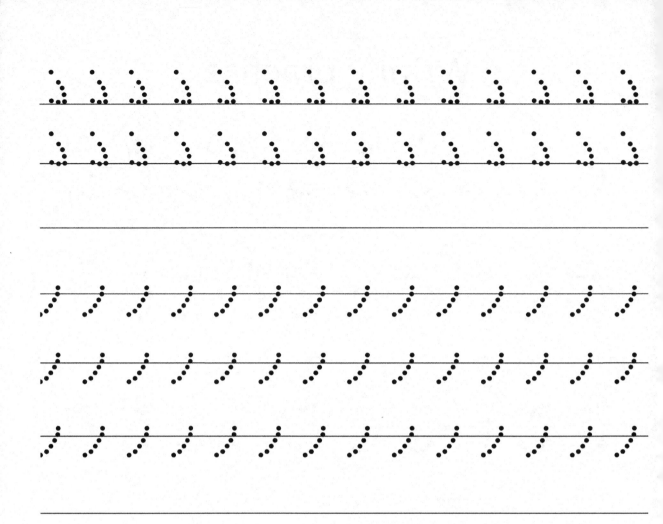

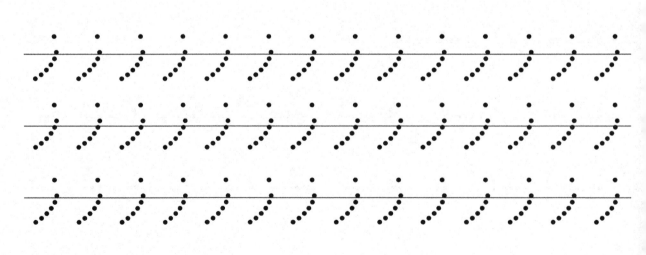

Section B: Conversation
Your name

أنا ليلا

ana layla

I am Layla.

شو أسميش

shu ismish?

What is your name?

أنا ميكل

ana Mikal

I am Mikael

شو أسمك؟

shu asmak??

What is your name?

You Tube Video: Lesson 1 part B, C

Vocabulary

English	Transliteration	Arabic
bread	khubz	خبز
chicken	dajaaj	دجاج
gold	dhahab	ذهب
man	rajul	رجل
fish	samaka	سمكة
giraffe	zaraafa	زرافة
what	shu	شو
your name	ashmish (to a girl)	أسميش
your name	asmak (to a boy)	أسمك
I	ana	أنا

Assessment : Lesson 1

Listen to your teacher and mark the letter with a X which he/she pronounce.

1	س	د	ذ	ر	خ	ز
2	ر	س	ز	خ	ذ	د
3	د	ز	س	خ	ذ	ر
4	ذ	خ	ز	س	ر	د
5	د	ز	س	ر	ذ	خ
6	ر	د	ذ	س	ز	خ
7	خ	ذ	د	ر	س	ز
8	ر	د	س	ذ	ز	خ

Assessment : Lesson 1+ 2

Listen to your teacher and mark the letter with a X which he/she pronounce.

1	ت	ج	س	خ	د	ر	ب
2	ز	ا	ذ	ج	خ	ث	ح
3	ج	ذ	ح	خ	ب		ت
4	ح	ب	س	د	ث	ج	خ
5	ج	ث	ا	ت	خ	س	ذ
6	ب	ز	ا	د	ح	ر	ث
7	ذ	ج	خ	س	د	ز	ت
8	د	ب	ر	خ	ذ	ت	ج
9	خ	ج	ب	ث	ح	س	ذ
10	ز	ح	ر	ذ	ا	س	ب

Assessment : Lesson 1+ 2

Listen to your teacher and mark the letter with a X which he/she pronounce.

| 1 | ت | ج | س | خ | د | ر | ب |

| 2 | ز | ا | ذ | ج | خ | ث | ح |

| 3 | ج | ذ | ح | خ | ب | ت |

| 4 | ح | ب | س | د | ث | ج | خ |

| 5 | ج | ث | ا | ت | خ | س | ذ |

| 6 | ب | ز | ا | د | ح | ر | ث |

| 7 | ذ | ج | خ | س | د | ز | ت |

| 8 | د | ب | ر | خ | ذ | ت | ج |

| 9 | خ | ج | ب | ث | ح | س | ذ |

| 10 | ز | ح | ر | ذ | ا | س | ب |

Lesson 3
Section A: Writing

	ﺶ	ش
	ﺺ	ص
	ﺾ	ض
	ﻂ	ط
	ﻆ	ظ
	ﻉ	ع

The Arabic Alphabet

Name: shiin **Pronunciation: 'sh' like in <u>sheep</u>**

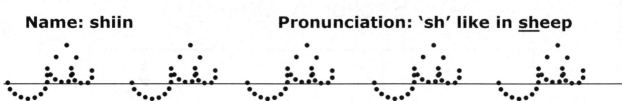

Write the shiin on the line below: (Remember: Start from the right side!)

Name: Saad **Pronunciation: a deep S-sound**

Write the Saad on the line below: (Remember: Start from the right side!)

Name: Daad **Pronunciation: a deep D-sound**

Write the daad on the line below: (Remember: Start from the right side!)

The Arabic Alphabet

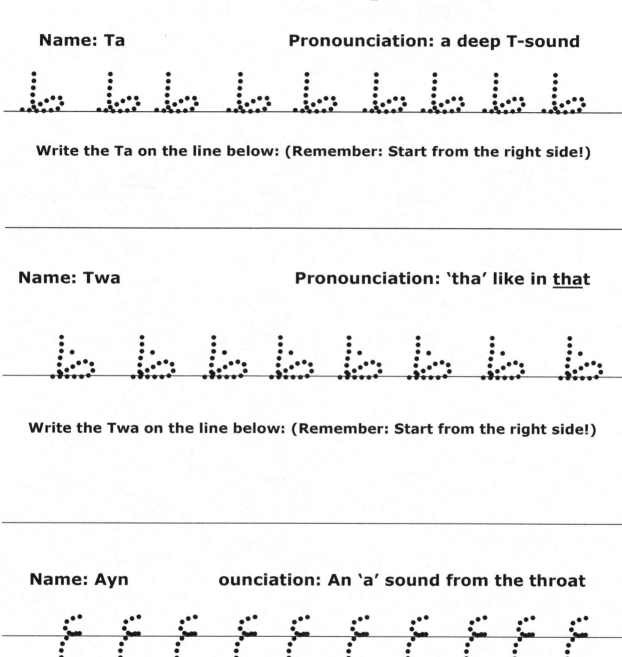

Name: Ta   **Pronounciation: a deep T-sound**

Write the Ta on the line below: (Remember: Start from the right side!)

Name: Twa   **Pronounciation: 'tha' like in <u>that</u>**

Write the Twa on the line below: (Remember: Start from the right side!)

Name: Ayn   **ounciation: An 'a' sound from the throat**

Write the Ayn on the line below: (Remember: Start from the right side!)

Exercise

Colour in the correct letter.

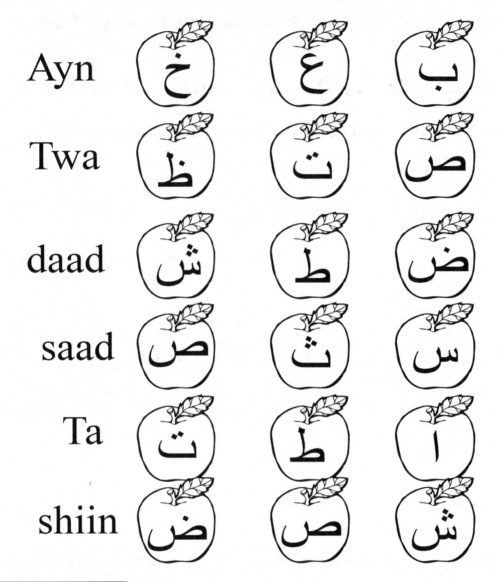

Ayn	خ	ع	ب
Twa	ظ	ت	ص
daad	ش	ط	ض
saad	ص	ث	س
Ta	ت	ط	ا
shiin	ض	ص	ش

You Tube Video:

Watch the youtube video below to see how we write and pronounce these letters.

2:56

Writing Arabic: The Alphabet Part 1

Writing Arabic: The alphabet Part 1

Writing Arabic: The alphabet Part 2

Just type 'marios arabic' at youtube search.

27

Exercise: Colouring

ش

shams
شمس

ص

sanduq
صندوق

ض

DufdA
ضفدع

ط

Taa'ira
طائرة

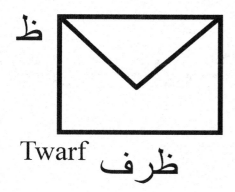

ظ

Twarf
ظرف

ع

Ayn
عين

28

Writing practise

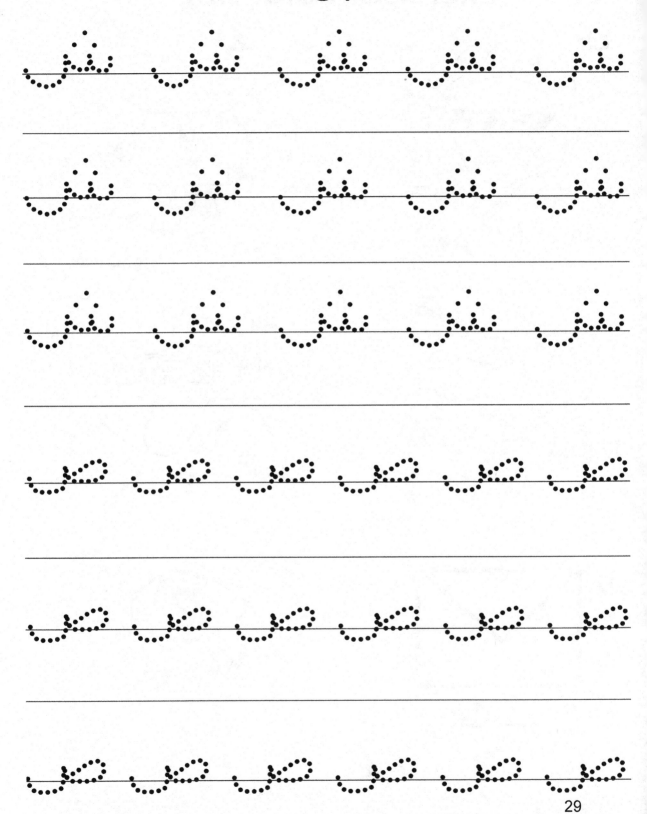

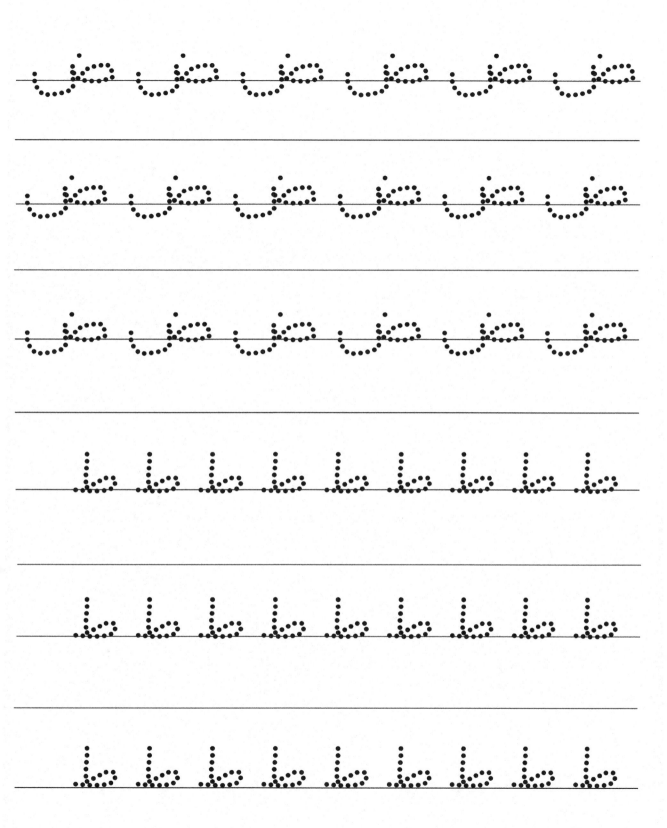

ҍ ҍ ҍ ҍ ҍ ҍ ҍ ҍ

ҍ ҍ ҍ ҍ ҍ ҍ ҍ ҍ

ҍ ҍ ҍ ҍ ҍ ҍ ҍ ҍ

ε ε ε ε ε ε ε ε ε ε ε ε

ε ε ε ε ε ε ε ε ε ε ε ε

ε ε ε ε ε ε ε ε ε ε ε ε

Section B: Conversation
Personal pronouns

Vocabulary

English	Transliteration	Arabic
sun	shams	شمس
box	sanduq	صندوق
frog	DufdA	ضفدع
airplane	Taa'ira	طائرة
envelope	Twarf	ظرف
eye	Ayn	عين
I	ana	أنا
you	anta (to a boy)	أنتَ
you	anti (to a girl)	أنتِ
he	huwwa	هو
she	hayya	هي
they	humma	هم
we	naHnu	نحن

Assessment : Lesson 3

Listen to your teacher and mark the letter with a X which he/she pronounce.

1 | ط | ص | ع | ظ | ش | ض |

2 | ظ | ض | ش | ع | ط | ص |

3 | ع | ص | ظ | ض | ش | ط |

4 | ض | ظ | ش | ط | ص | ع |

5 | ظ | ص | ط | ع | ش | ض |

6 | ص | ض | ط | ش | ع | ظ |

7 | ض | ش | ع | ط | ظ | ص |

8 | ع | ط | ص | ظ | ض | ش |

Assessment : Lesson 1+ 2 + 3

Listen to your teacher and mark the letter with a X which he/she pronounce.

#							
1	ب	ر	ص	خ	س	ش	ت
2	ح	ث	خ	ج	ذ	ض	ز
3	ت	ع	ب	خ	ح	ذ	ج
4	خ	ج	ع	د	س	ط	ح
5	ذ	س	ظ	ت	ا	ض	ط
6	ث	ر	ح	د	ص	ش	ب
7	ت	ص	د	س	ش	ج	ذ
8	ج	ت	ذ	خ	ض	ب	د
9	ذ	س	ط	ث	ب	ج	خ
10	ب	ا	ظ	ر	ح	ص	س

Lesson 4
Section A: Writing

	ع	غ
	ف	ف
	ق	ق
	ك	ك
	ل	ل
	م	م

The Arabic Alphabet

Name: ghayn **Pronunciation: a gargle sound**

Write the ghayn on the line below: (Remember: Start from the right side!)

Name: fa **Pronunciation: 'f' like in f̲loor**

Write the fa on the line below: (Remember: Start from the right side!)

Name: qaaf **Pronunciation: a k-sound from the throat**

Write the qaaf on the line below: (Remember: Start from the right side!)

The Arabic Alphabet

Name: kaaf **Pronunciation: 'k' like in keeper**

Write the kaaf on the line below: (Remember: Start from the right side!)

Name: laam **Pronunciation: 'l' like in long**

ل ل ل ل ل ل ل

Write the fa on the line below: (Remember: Start from the right side!)

Name: miim **Pronunciation: 'm' like in more**

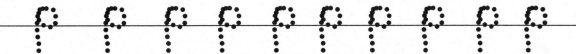

Write the miim on the line below: (Remember: Start from the right side!)

Exercise

a) Draw a ▢ around the ghayn.

b) Draw a △ around the fa.

c) Draw a ◯ around the qaaf.

d) Draw a ◇ around the kaaf.

e) Draw a ☆ around the laam.

f) Draw a ⬡ around the miim.

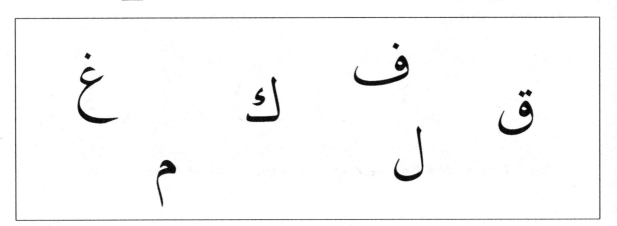

غ   ك   ف   ق

م   ل

You Tube Videos:

Watch the youtube video below to see how we write and pronounce these letters.

Writing Arabic: The Alphabet Part 1

Writing Arabic: The alphabet Part 1
Writing Arabic: The alphabet Part 2

Just type 'marios arabic'
at youtube search.

Exercise: Colouring

غ

ghuraab غراب

ف

fawaaka
فواكة

ق

qamr قمر

ك

kalb كلب

ل

lemon ليمون

م

masjid مسجد

Writing practise

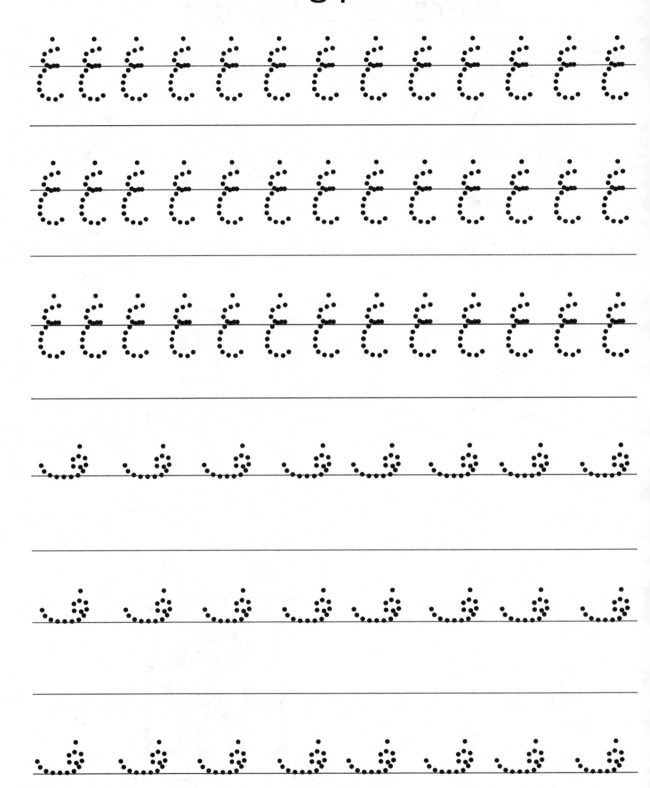

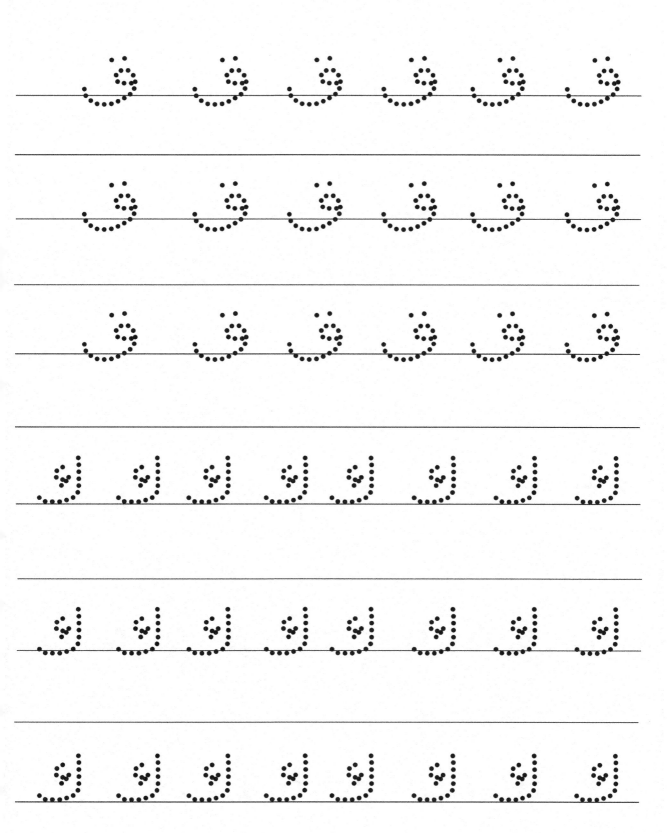

42

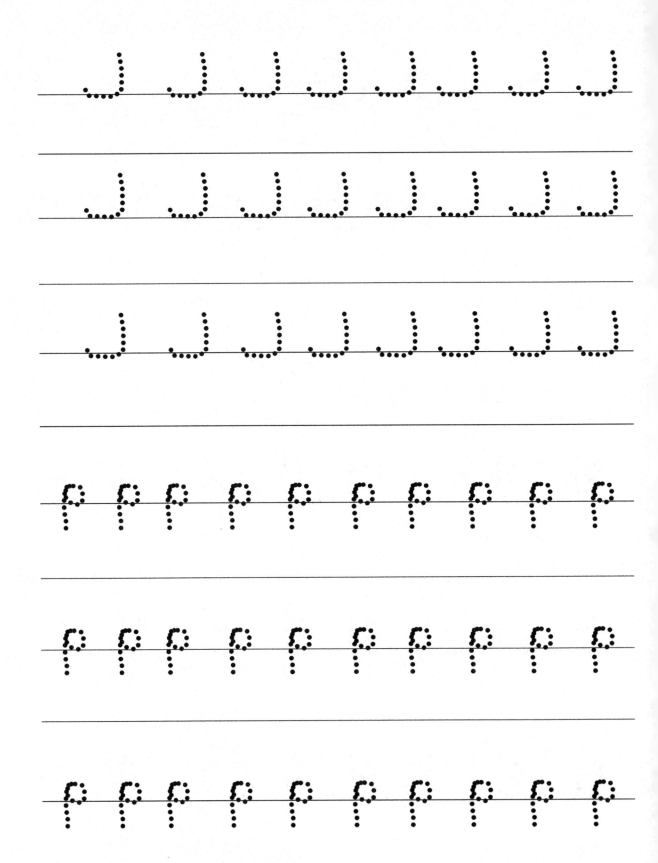

43

Section B: Conversation
Nouns 1

فنجان finjaan
cup

كتاب kitaab
book

باب bab
door

قميص qamiis
shirt

ساعة saaA
clock

كرسي kursi
chair

طاولة Taula
table

دفتر notebook diftar

مفتاح muftaaH
key

قلم qalm
pen

Vocabulary

English	Transliteration	Arabic
crow	ghuraab	غراب
fruit	fawaaka	فواكه
moon	qamr	قمر
dog	kalb	كلب
lemon	liimun	ليمون
mosque	masjid	مسجد
book	kitaab	كتاب
cup	finjaan	فنجان
chair	kursi	كرسي
shirt	qamiiS	قميص
clock	saaA	ساعة
key	muftaaH	مفتاح
table	Taula	طاولة

Vocabulary

English	Transliteration	Arabic
notebook	diftar	دفتر
pen	qalm	قلم

Assessment : Lesson 4

Listen to your teacher and mark the letter with a X which he/she pronounce.

1 | ك | ف | ق | غ | ل | م |

2 | ق | ك | غ | ف | م | ل |

3 | ف | ل | ك | غ | م | ق |

4 | ك | م | ف | ل | ق | غ |

5 | ل | ق | غ | ك | م | ف |

6 | ق | ف | ك | م | غ | ل |

7 | غ | ق | ل | ك | ف | م |

8 | ك | م | ف | ل | غ | ق |

Assessment : Lesson 1 + 2 + 3 + 4

Listen to your teacher and mark the letter with a X which he/she pronounce.

1	ت	ش	غ	خ	ص	ر	ب
2	ز	ض	ذ	ج	ف	ث	ح
3	ج	ق	ح	خ	ب	ع	ت
4	ح	ط	س	ك	ع	ج	خ
5	ط	ل	ا	ت	ظ	س	ذ
6	ب	ش	ص	م	ح	ر	ث
7	ذ	ج	غ	س	د	ص	ت
8	د	ب	ك	خ	ذ	ت	ق
9	خ	ج	ل	ث	ط	س	ذ
10	ص	ح	غ	ظ	ا	س	ب

Assessment : Nouns 1

Listen to your teacher and mark the picture with a X which he/she says.

Assessment : Nouns 1

Listen to your teacher and mark the picture with a X which he/she says.

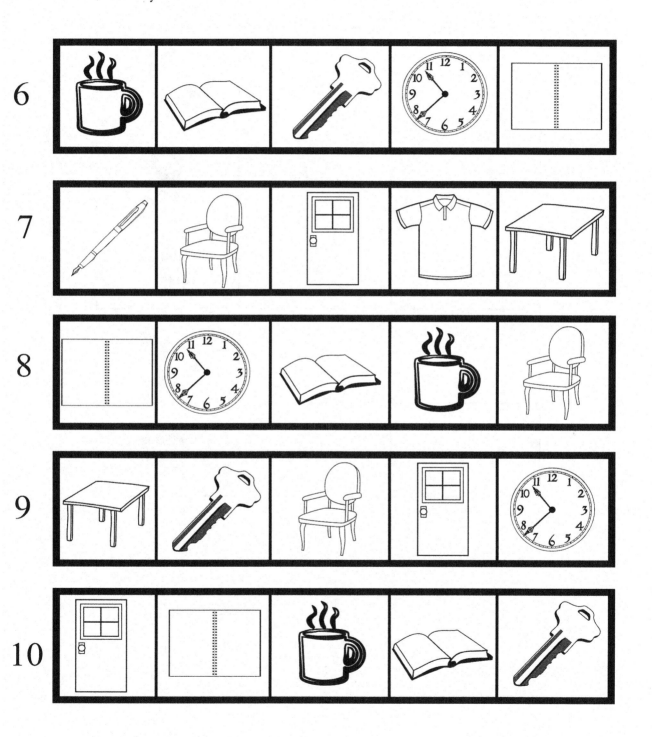

Lesson 5
Section A: Writing

	﬜	نـ
	○	ة
	ﻭ	و
	ﻳ	ي
	ﻋ	ع

The Arabic Alphabet

Name: nun   **Pronunciation: like the 'n' in <u>no</u>**

Write the nun on the line below: (Remember: Start from the right side!)

Name: he   **Pronunciation: 'h' like in <u>horse</u>**

Write the he on the line below: (Remember: Start from the right side!)

Name: waw   **Pronunciation: Like the 'w' in <u>winner</u> or**
                                   Like the "oo" in s<u>oo</u>n

Write the waw on the line below: (Remember: Start from the right side!)

The Arabic Alphabet

Name: ya   **Pronounciation:**   Like the "y" in yes or
                                                Like the "ee" in seen

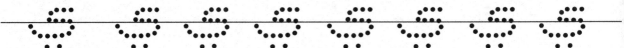

Write the ya on the line below: (Remember: Start from the right side!)

Name: hamza   **Pronounciation:**   a stop–sound like in oh–oh

---

Write the hamza on the line below: (Remember: Start from the right side!)

Most of the time we write the hamza on the alif, waw and ya.
Practise writing the hamza on these letters on the lines below:

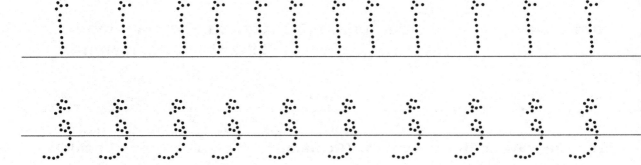

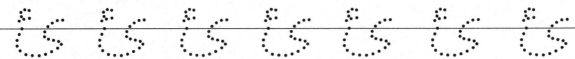

53

Exercise

Colour in the correct letter.

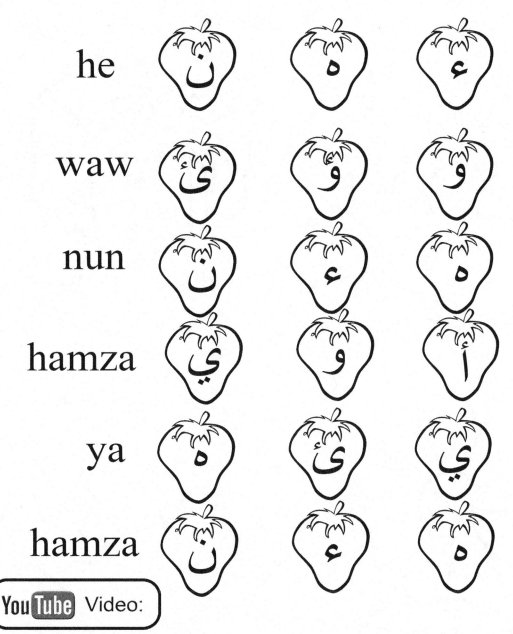

he	نْ	ه	ع
waw	ئ	و	وَ
nun	نْ	ع	ه
hamza	ي	و	ا
ya	ه	ئ	ي
hamza	نْ	ع	ه

You Tube Video:

Watch the youtube video below to see how we write and pronounce these letters.

Writing Arabic: The alphabet Part 1
Writing Arabic: The alphabet Part 2

2:56

Writing Arabic: The Alphabet
Part 1

Just type 'marios arabic'
at youtube search.

Exercise: Colouring

ن

naar نار

ه

hadiya هديّة

و

warda وردة

م

yad يد

Writing practise

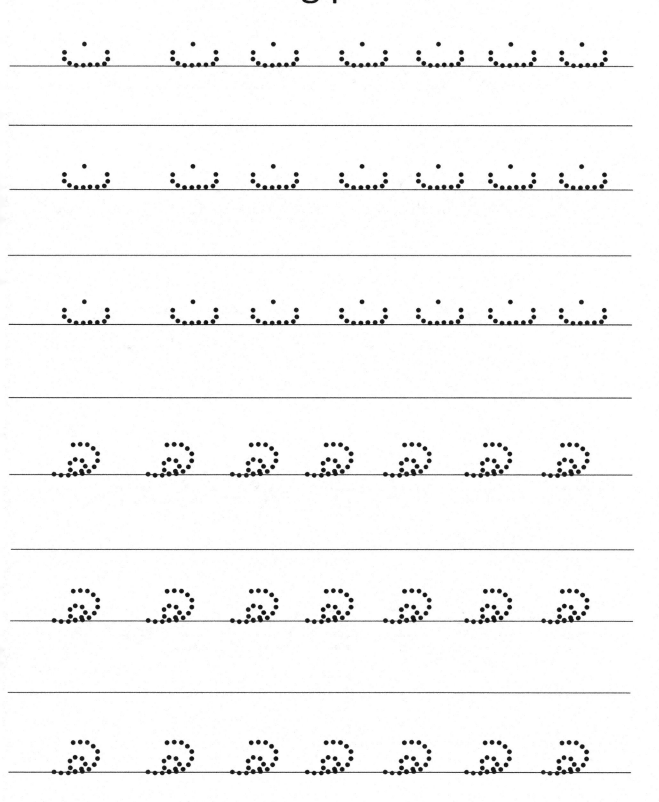

Writing practise

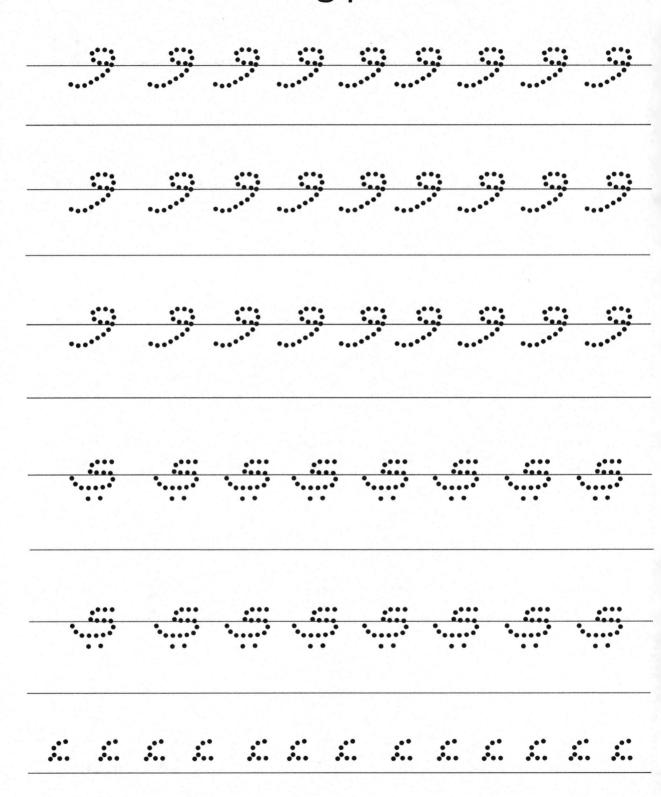

Section B: Conversation
Action words

يشرب ماء
yishrab ma'

يجري
yijree

He runs.

يمشي
yimshee

He walks.

He drinks water.

يضرب كرة
yuDrab kora

يفتح الباب
yiftaH albaab

يلبس قميص
yilbas qamiis

He opens the door.

He hits a ball.

He puts on a shirt.

يكتب كتاب
yiktib kitaab.

He writes a book.

You Tube Video: Lesson 3 : Action words 1

Vocabulary

English	Transliteration	Arabic
fire	naar	نار
gift	hadiyya	هديّة
flower	warda	وردة
hand	yad	يد
he walks	yimshii	يمشي
he runs	yijrii	يجري
he drinks	yishrab	يشرب
water	maa'	ماء
he hits	yuDrub	يضرب
ball	koora	كرة
he opens	yiftaH	يفتح
he writes	yiktib	يكتب
he puts on	yilbas	يلبس

Assessment : Lesson 5

Listen to your teacher and mark the letter with a X which he/she pronounce.

1	ه	و	ي	ء	ن	ئ

2	و	ه	ئ	ن	ء	ي

3	ء	ي	ه	و	ن	أ

4	ن	ئ	ي	ه	و	ؤ

5	و	ؤ	ه	ي	ن	ء

6	أ	ن	ي	و	ء	ه

7	ه	ي	ن	و	ئ	أ

8	و	ن	أ	ئ	ه	ي

Assessment : All letters

Listen to your teacher and mark the letter with a X which he/she pronounce.

1	ت	ي	غ	خ	ص	ر	ب
2	ح	ث	ف	أ	ذ	ض	و
3	ت	ع	ب	خ	ه	ق	ج
4	ئ	ج	ع	ن	س	ط	ح
5	ذ	س	ه	ت	ا	ل	ط
6	ث	ر	ح	م	و	ش	ب
7	ت	ص	د	س	غ	ي	ذ
8	ق	ت	ذ	خ	ك	ب	د
9	ذ	س	ط	ث	ل	ج	خ
10	ب	س	ا	ظ	غ	ح	ص

Assessment : Action Words 1

Listen to your teacher and mark the picture with a X which he/she says.

Assessment : Action Words 1

Listen to your teacher and mark the picture with a X which he/she says.

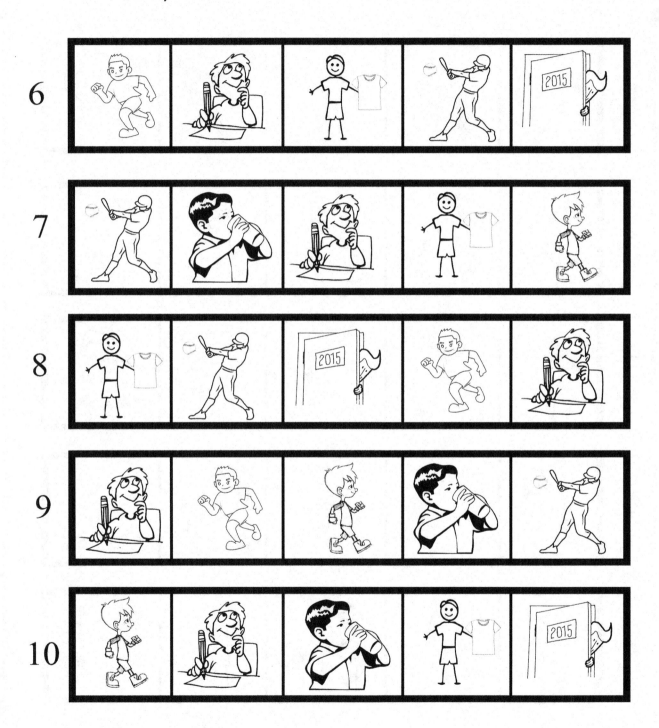

Lesson 6
Section A
Revision: Arabic Alphabet

Read the Arabic alphabet out loud.

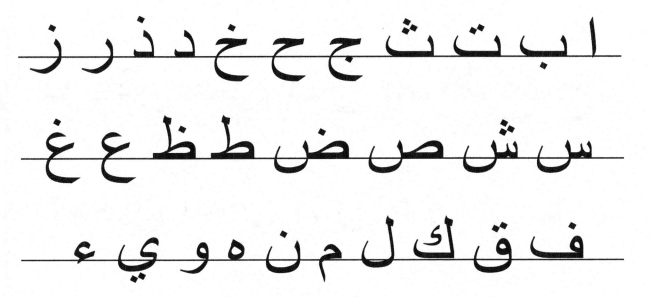

Trace the letters below.

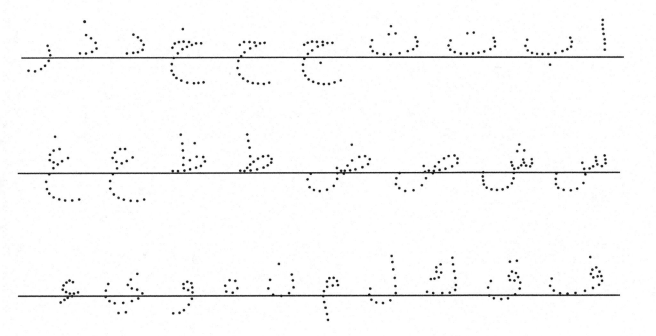

The Arabic alphabet with English sounds.

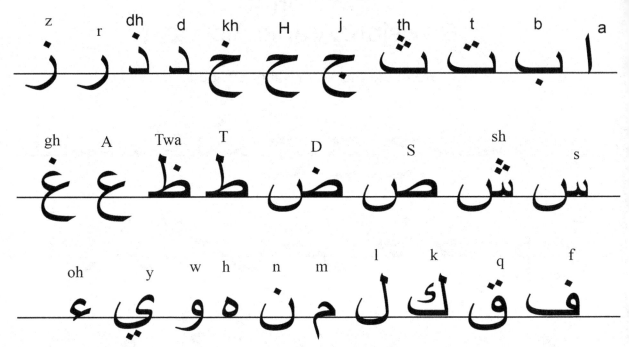

Write in the missing letters of the Arabic alphabet.

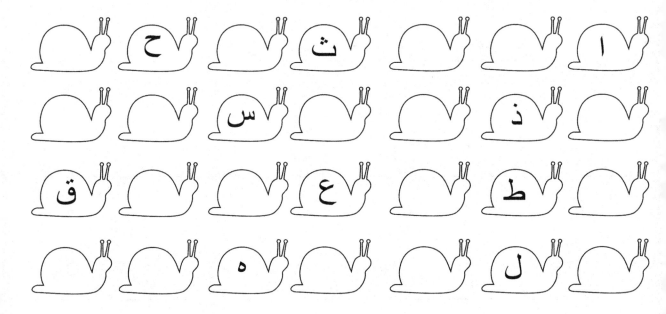

Exercise

Match the sound with the letter:

aa = ن ا ك

b = ب ع ث

t = ح غ ت

th = ث ش ص

j = ل ج خ

H = خ ح ج

Exercise

Match the sound with the letter:

kh = خ   ح   ج

d = ر   ز   د

dh = ط   ه   ذ

r = غ   ر   ز

z = ظ   ض   ز

s = ص   س   ش

Exercise

Match the sound with the letter:

sh =   ش   ص   س

S =   ض   ص   ق

D =   د   ذ   ض

T =   ط   ظ   ت

Twa =   ث   ف   ظ

A =   غ   ع   ق

Exercise

Match the sound with the letter:

gh = ق   غ   ف

f = ف   ق   غ

q = خ   ف   ق

k = ق   ك   ل

l = ل   ك   غ

m = ب   م   ي

Exercise

Match the sound with the letter:

n = ث   ب   ن

h = ح   ه   ا

w = و   ئ   ؤ

y = ي   ت   م

oh = ء   ك   غ

Section B: Conversation
Prepositions

وين الفنجان؟

الفنجان على الطولة

alfinjaan Ale aTTaula

on

الفنجان أمام الطولة

alfinjaan amaam aTTaula

above

in front of

behind

الفنجان فوق الطولة

alfinjaan foq aTTaula

الفنجان خلف الطولة

alfinjaan khalf aTTaula

under

next to

الفنجان تحت الطولة

alfinjaan taHt aTTaula

الفنجان بجانب الطولة

alfinjaan bijanb aTTaula

You Tube Video: Lesson 4 : Prepositions

Exercise

Write the number of the correct sentence on the table in the picture.

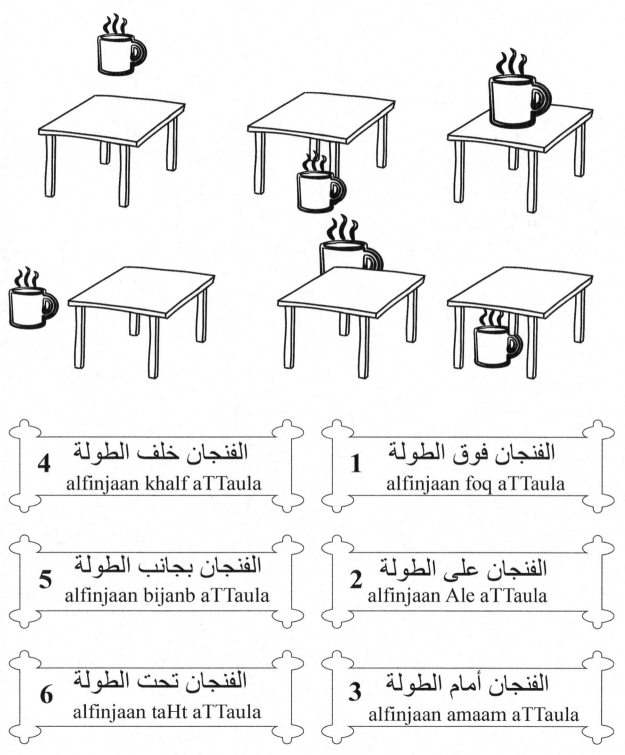

4	الفنجان خلف الطولة alfinjaan khalf aTTaula	1	الفنجان فوق الطولة alfinjaan foq aTTaula
5	الفنجان بجانب الطولة alfinjaan bijanb aTTaula	2	الفنجان على الطولة alfinjaan Ale aTTaula
6	الفنجان تحت الطولة alfinjaan taHt aTTaula	3	الفنجان أمام الطولة alfinjaan amaam aTTaula

Exercise

Colour the duck and the flower with the same color which have the same meaning.

Vocabulary

English	Transliteration	Arabic
where	ween	وين
the	al	ال
cup	finjaan	فنجان
table	Taula	طاولة
on	Ale	على
next to	bijaanib	بجانب
under	taHt	تحت
behind	khalf	خلف
above	foq	فوق
in front of	amaam	أمام

Assessment : All letters

Listen to your teacher and mark the letter with a X which he/she pronounce.

1	ب	ر	ص	خ	غ	ي	ت

2	ح	ث	ف	أ	ذ	ض	و

3	ت	ع	ب	خ	ه	ق	ج

4	ئ	ج	ع	ن	س	ط	ح

5	ذ	س	ه	ت	ا	ل	ط

6	ث	ر	ح	م	و	ش	ب

7	ت	ص	د	س	غ	ي	ذ

8	ق	ت	ذ	خ	ك	ب	د

9	ذ	س	ط	ث	ل	ج	خ

10	ب	س	ا	ظ	غ	ح	ص

Assessment : Prepositions

Listen to your teacher and mark the picture with a X which he/she says.

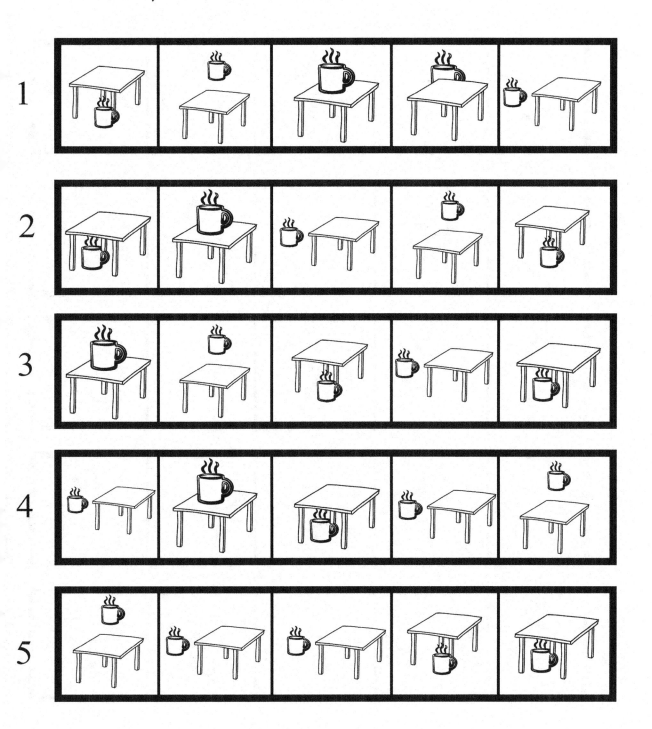

Assessment : Prepositions

Listen to your teacher and mark the picture with a X which he/she says.

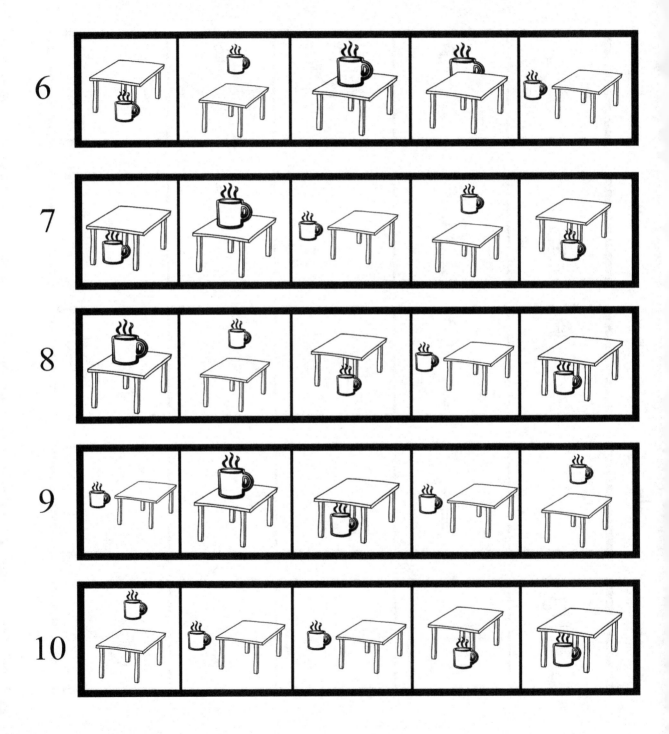

Lesson 7
Section A
Vowels

There are 3 vowels in Arabic. These vowels are the 'a', 'i' and 'u' sound.
The 'a' is written on top of the letters. It looks like a small dash.

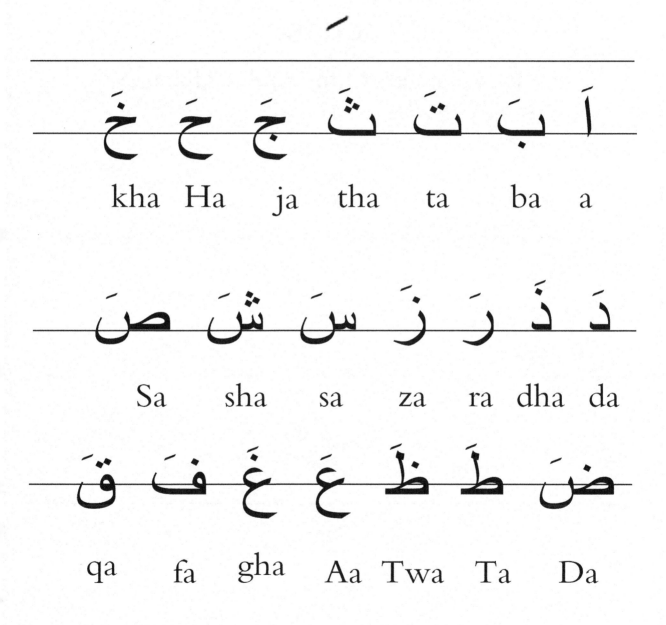

kha Ha ja tha ta ba a

Sa sha sa za ra dha da

qa fa gha Aa Twa Ta Da

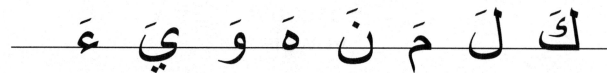

a' ya wa ha na ma la ka

Practise:

Trace the letters of the Arabic alphabet below with the 'a'-vowel.

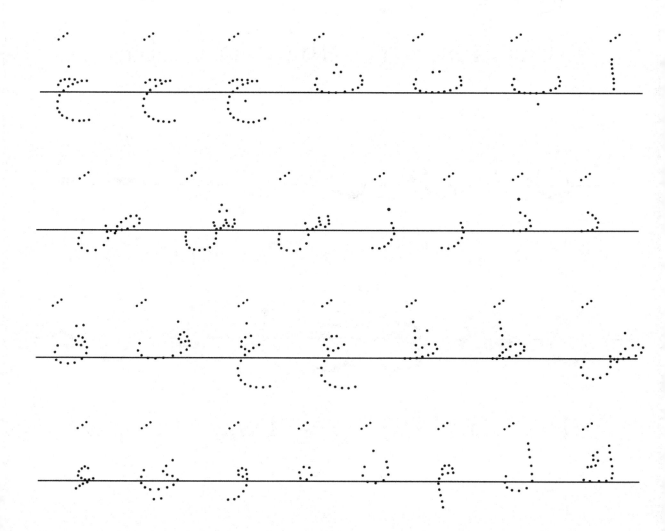

Exercise

Colour the Arabic letters accoring to the sounds below:

aa - yellow	dha - green	Twa- purple	na- brown
ba - brown	ra - pink	Aa- black	ha- red
ta - red	za - yellow	gha - white	wa- blue
tha - blue	sa - brown	fa - white	ya- orange
ja - orange	sha - red	qa - green	a'- purple
Ha - purple	Sa- blue	ka - pink	
kha - black	Da- orange	la- yellow	
da - white	Ta- yellow	ma- brown	

80

Section B: Conversation
My family

من هو؟ min huwwa Who is he?

من هي؟ min hayya Who is she?

أخي akhi — my brother

ابي abbi — my father

أختي ukhti — my sister

أمي ummi — my mother

جدتي jidditi — my grandmother

جدي jiddi — my grandfather

YouTube Video: Lesson 5 : Talking about my family

Exercise

Connect the words with the pictures.

أختي
ukhti

جدتي
jidditi

أمي
ummi

ابي
abbi

أخي
akhi

جدي
jiddi

Vocabulary

English	Transliteration	Arabic
my brother	ummi	أخي
my sister	ukhti	أختي
my mother	finjaan	أمي
my father	abbi	ابي
my grandmother	jidditi	جدتي
my grandfather	jiddi	جدي

Assessment : All letters

Listen to your teacher and mark the letter with a X which
he/she pronounce.

1	تَ	يَ	غَ	خَ	صَ	رَ	بَ
2	وَ	ضَ	ذَ	أَ	فَ	ثَ	حَ
3	جَ	قَ	هَ	خَ	بَ	عَ	تَ
4	حَ	طَ	سَ	نَ	عَ	جَ	ئَ
5	طَ	لَ	اَ	تَ	هَ	سَ	ذَ
6	بَ	شَ	وَ	مَ	حَ	رَ	ثَ
7	ذَ	يَ	غَ	سَ	دَ	صَ	تَ
8	دَ	بَ	كَ	خَ	ذَ	تَ	قَ
9	خَ	جَ	لَ	ثَ	طَ	سَ	ذَ
10	صَ	حَ	غَ	ظَ	اَ	سَ	بَ

84

Assessment : Family

Listen to your teacher and mark the picture with a X which he/she says.

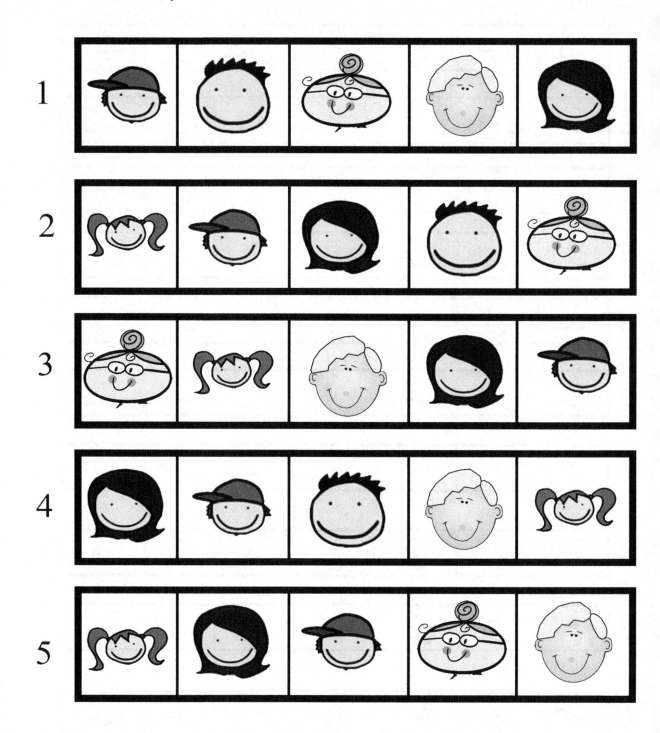

Assessment : Family

Listen to your teacher and mark the picture with a X which he/she says.

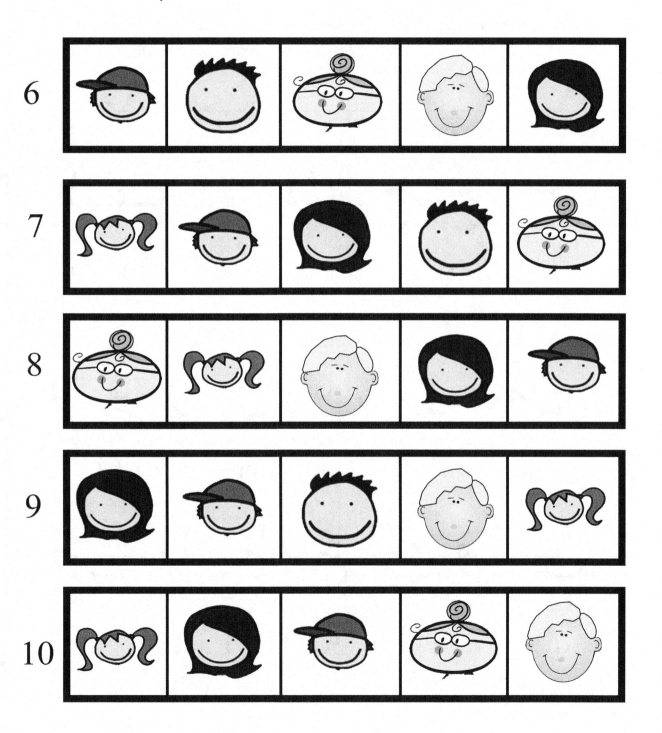

6

7

8

9

10

Lesson 8
Section A
Vowels

There are 3 vowels in Arabic. These vowels are the 'a', 'i' and 'u' sound.
The 'i' is written at the bottom of the letters. It looks like a small dash
under each letter.

khi   Hi   ji   thi   ti   bi   i

Si   shi   si   zi   ri   dhi   di

qi   fi   ghi   Ai   Twi   Ti   Di

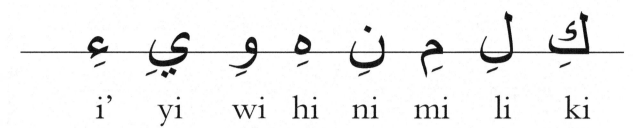

i' yi wi hi ni mi li ki

Practise:

Trace the letters of the Arabic alphabet below with the 'i'-vowel.

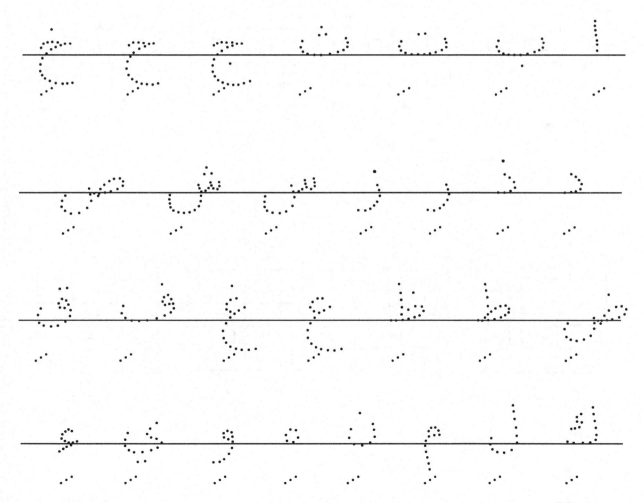

Exercise

Conect the sound to the Arabic letter through each maze.

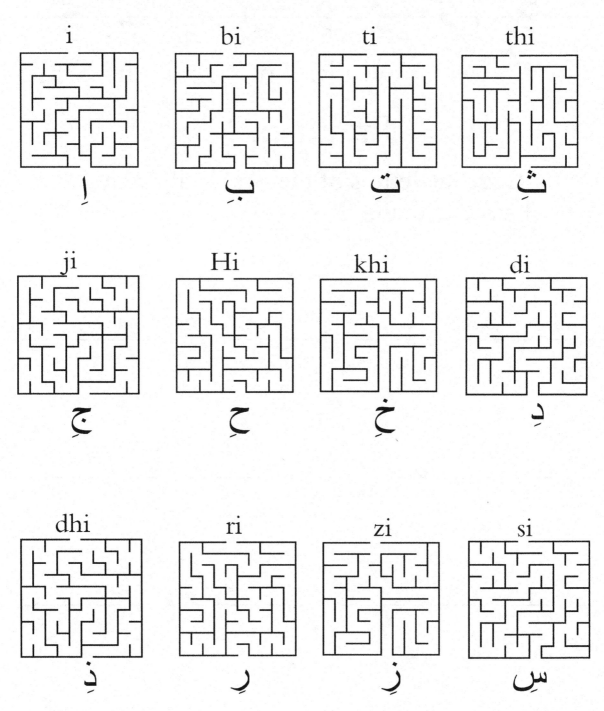

i

bi

ti

thi

ا

بِ

تِ

ثِ

ji

Hi

khi

di

جِ

حِ

خِ

دِ

dhi

ri

zi

si

ذِ

رِ

زِ

سِ

Exercise

Connect the sound to the Arabic letter through each maze.

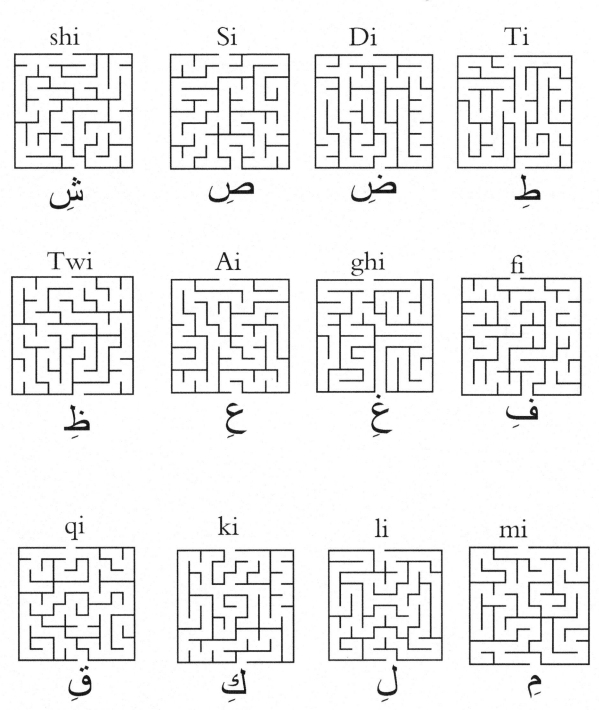

shi   Si   Di   Ti

شِ   صِ   ضِ   طِ

Twi   Ai   ghi   fi

ظِ   عِ   غِ   فِ

qi   ki   li   mi

قِ   كِ   لِ   مِ

Exercise

Connect the sound to the Arabic letter through each maze.

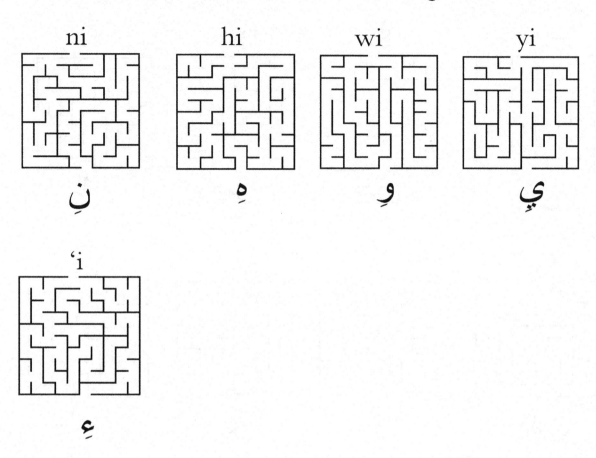

ni   hi   wi   yi

نِ   هِ   وِ   يِ

'i

ءِ

Section B: Conversation
Places

مسجد

masjid

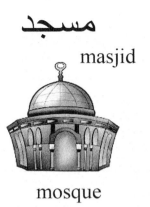

mosque

بيت

bayt

house

خيمة

khayma

tent

حديقة الحياونات

Hadiqat alHayaawanaat

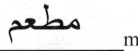

zoo

مدرسة

madrassa

school

مطعم

maTAam

restaurant

مستشفة

mustashfa

hospital

You**Tube**   Video: Lesson 6: Talking about places

Exercise

Choose the correct annswer. Make a cross over A, B or C.

ween jiddi? وين جدي؟

amaam almasjid	أمام المسجد	A
amaam almasjid	تحت المسجد	B
amaam almasjid	فوق المسجد	C

ween ummi? وين أمي؟

khalf alkhayma	خلف الخيمة	A
amaam alkhayma	أمام الخيمة	B
bijaanib alkhayma	بجانب الخيمة	C

ween akhi? وين أخي؟

taHt albayt	تحت البيت	A
foq albayt	فوق البيت	B
bijaanib albayt	بجانب البيت	C

ween ukhti? وين أختي؟

khalf almadrassa	خلف المدرسة	A
taHt almadrassa	تحت المدرسة	B
amaam almadrassa	أمام المدرسة	C

Exercise

Choose the correct annswer. Make a cross over A, B or C.

ween jidditi?   وين جدتي؟

amaam almasjid	أمام المستشفة	A
amaam almasjid	تحت المستشفة	B
amaam almasjid	فوق المستشفة	C

ween abbi?   وين ابي؟

خلف حديقة الحياونات khalf hadiqat alhayawanaat		A
فوق حديقة الحياونات foq hadiqat alhayawanaat		B
بجانب حديقة الحياونات bijaanib hadiqat alhayawanaat		C

ween ukhti?   وين أخي؟

khalf almAatam	خلف المطعم	A
amaam almAatam	أمام المطعم	B
taHt almAatam	تحت المطعم	C

Vocabulary

English	Transliteration	Arabic
where	ween	وين
the	al	ال
mosque	masjid	مسجد
house	bayt	بيت
hospital	mustashfa	مستشفة
tent	khayma	خيمة
restaurant	maTAam	مطعم
zoo	Hadiqat Alhayawanaat	حديقة الحياونات
school	madrassa	مدرسة

Assessment : All letters

Listen to your teacher and mark the letter with a X which he/she pronounce.

1	كِ	صِ	سِ	ثِ	فِ	قِ	اِ
2	بِ	ضِ	رِ	قِ	مِ	غِ	هِ
3	ثِ	يِ	خِ	عِ	تِ	ضِ	شِ
4	غِ	دِ	فِ	رِ	شِ	عِ	وِ
5	حِ	خِ	جِ	شِ	ءِ	لِ	نِ
6	نِ	تِ	ثِ	بِ	فِ	يِ	صِ
7	هِ	ضِ	شِ	قِ	تِ	سِ	غِ
8	لِ	كِ	حِ	ضِ	ذِ	طِ	مِ
9	ظِ	يِ	بِ	قِ	خِ	ثِ	صِ
10	غِ	نِ	شِ	خِ	وِ	تِ	فِ

Assessment : Places

Listen to your teacher and mark the picture with a X which he/she says.

Assessment : Places

Listen to your teacher and mark the picture with a X which he/she says.

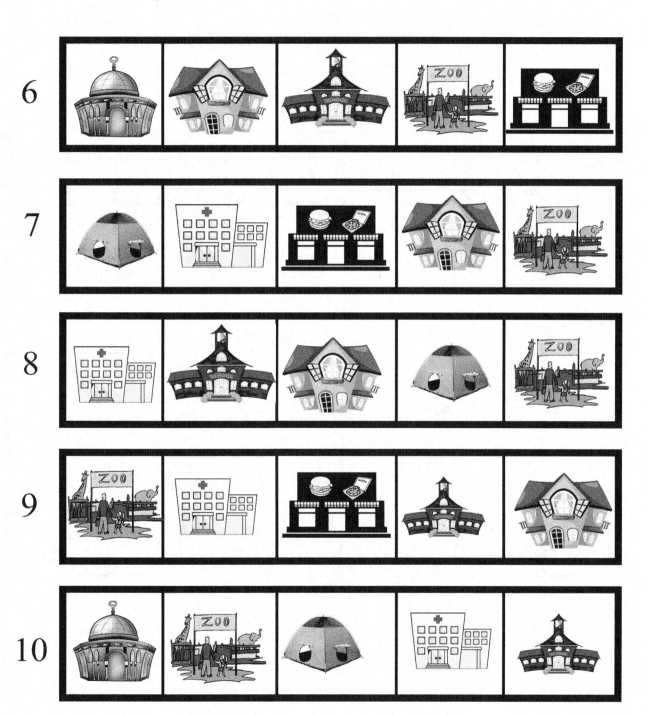

Lesson 9
Section A
Vowels

There are 3 vowels in Arabic. These vowels are the 'a', 'i' and 'u' sound.
The 'u' is written on top of the letters. It looks like a small dash
above each letter.

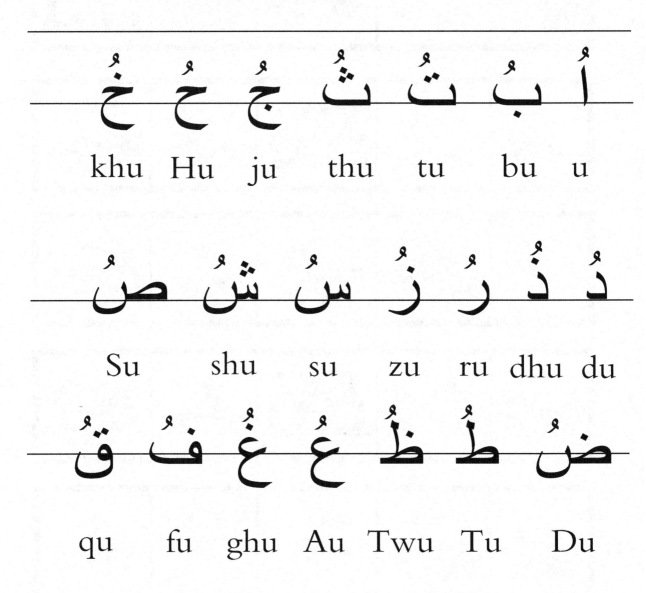

khu   Hu   ju   thu   tu   bu   u

Su   shu   su   zu   ru   dhu   du

qu   fu   ghu   Au   Twu   Tu   Du

كُ لُ مُ نُ هُ وُ يُ ءُ

u' yu wu hu nu mu lu ku

Practise:

Trace the letters of the Arabic alphabet below with the 'u'-vowel.

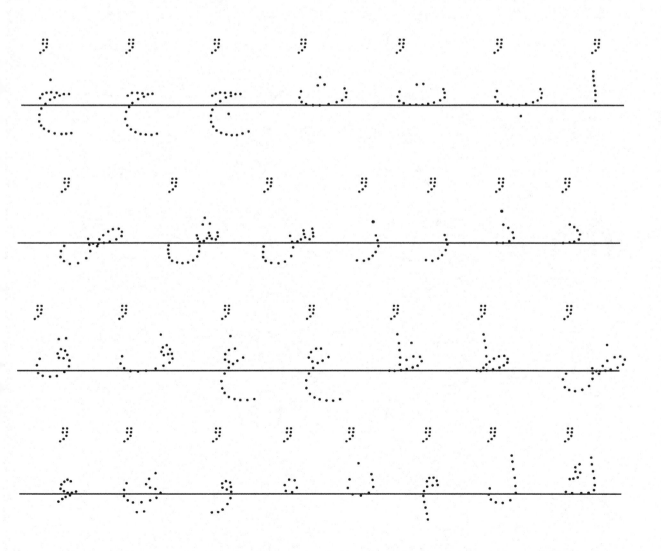

Exercise

Conect the sound to the Arabic letter through each maze.

u = ا ﺃ ﺇ

ba = ﺑُ ﺏ ﺏ

ti = ﺕ ﺕُ ﺕ

tha = ﺙ ﺙ ﺙُ

ji = ﺝ ﺝُ ﺝ

Hu = ﺡُ ﺡ ﺡ

Exercise

Conect the sound to the Arabic letter through each maze.

khi = خِ خُ خْ

di = دُ دْ دَ

dhu = ذَ ذُ ذْ

ri = رْ رَ رُ

zi = زَ زُ زِ

su = سُ سِ سَ

Exercise

Conect the sound to the Arabic letter through each maze.

khi = خِ   خُ   خَ

di = دُ   دَ   دِ

dhu = ذَ   ذُ   ذِ

ri = رَ   رِ   رُ

zi = زَ   زُ   زِ

su = سُ   سَ   سِ

Exercise

Colour the flower that matches the sound.

shu = ـشِ   شُ   شْ

Sa = صُ   صَ   صِ

Di = ضَ   ضُ   ضِ

Tu = طَ   طَ   طُ

Twi = ظْ   ظُ   ظْ

Ai = عُ   عَ   عِ

Exercise

Colour the flower that matches the sound.

gha =   غَ   غُ   غِ

fu =   فُ   فَ   فِ

qi =   قَ   قُ   قِ

ka =   كِ   كَ   كُ

li =   لَ   لُ   لِ

mu =   مُ   مِ   مَ

Exercise

Colour the flower that matches the sound.

ni = نِ نُ نَ

ha = هُ ه ه

wi = وَ وُ وِ

ya = يِ ي يُ

'i = ئ ئُ ئ

Section B: Conversation
Emotions

عطشان
AaTshaan
thirsty

خائف
khaa'if
afraid

خجلان
khajlaan
shy

مرتاح
murtaaH
comfortable

زعلان
zAlaan

فرحان
farHaan
happy

حزين
Haziin
sad

جوعان
juaan
hungry

You Tube   Video: Lesson 7: Part 1: Emotions : He

Exersize

Tick  the correct box.

جوعان
juaan

زعلان
zAlaan

مرتاح
murtaaH

حزين
Haziin

عطشان
AaTshaan

Exersize

Tick  the correct box.

خائف
khaa'if

خجلان
khajlaan

عطشان
AaTshaan

زعلان
zAlaan

فرحان
farHaan

Vocabulary

English	Transliteration	Arabic
afraid	khaa'if	خائف
hungry	juAaan	جوعان
thirsty	AaTshaan	عطشان
sad	Haziin	حزين
angry	zAlaan	زعلان
comfortable	murtaaH	مرتاح
shy	khashlaan	خجلان
happy	farHaan	فرحان

Assessment : Emotions

Listen to your teacher and mark the picture with a X which he/she says.

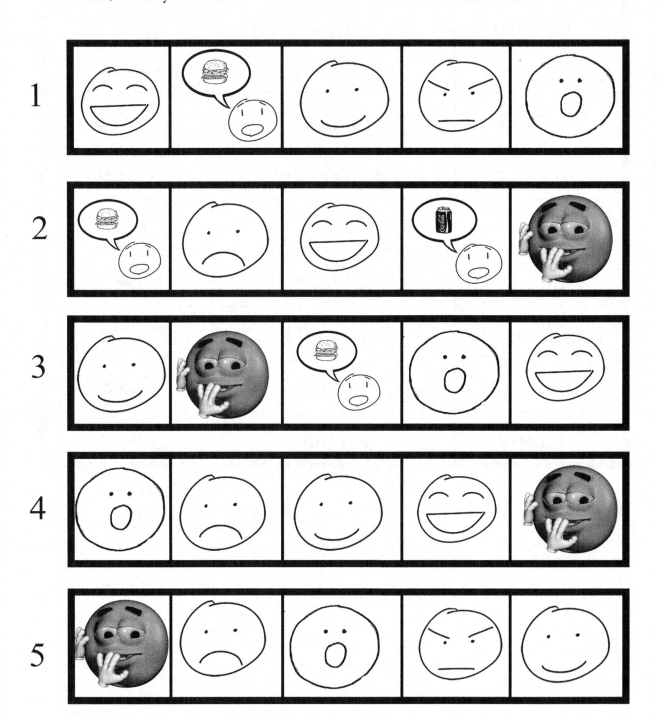

Assessment : Emotions

Listen to your teacher and mark the picture with a X which he/she says.

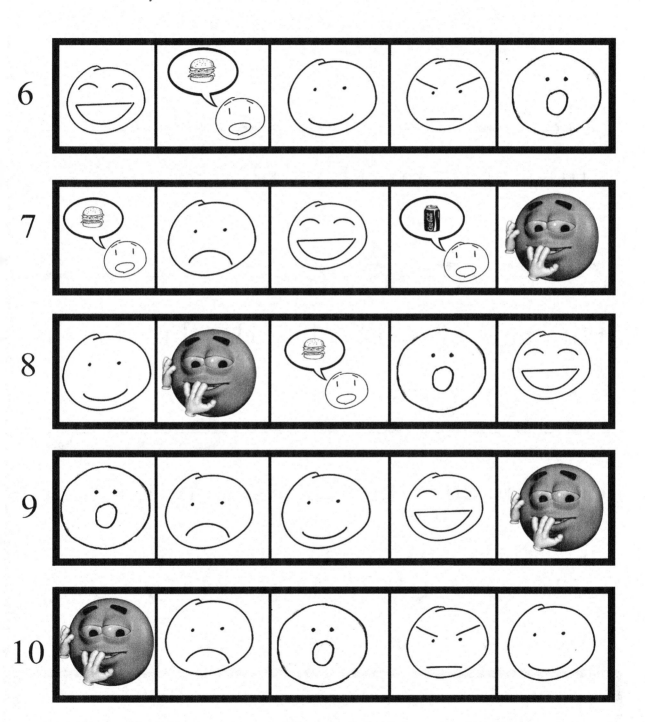

Lesson 10
Section A
Reading the Alphabet with the vowels.

Read the Arabic Alphabet below with the vowels.
If you need help, watch the youtube videos below.

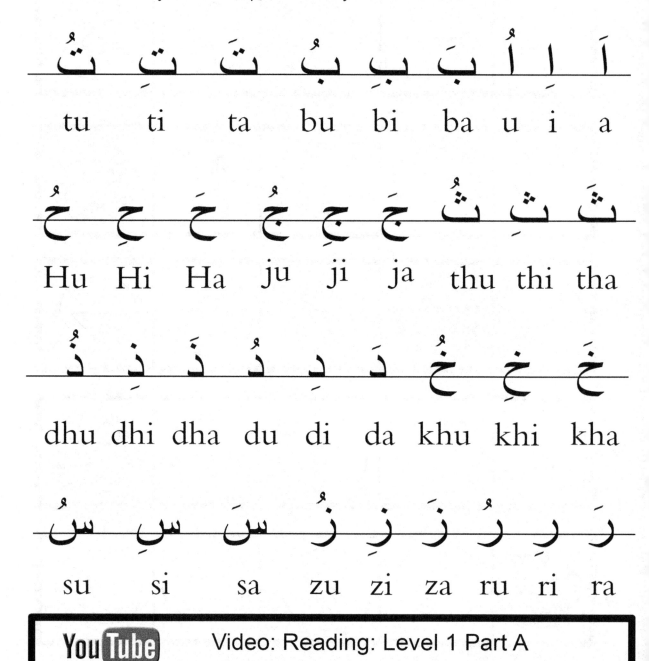

اَ   اِ   اُ   بَ   بِ   بُ   تَ   تِ   تُ

a   i   u   ba   bi   bu   ta   ti   tu

ثَ   ثِ   ثُ   جَ   جِ   جُ   حَ   حِ   حُ

tha   thi   thu   ja   ji   ju   Ha   Hi   Hu

خَ   خِ   خُ   دَ   دِ   دُ   ذَ   ذِ   ذُ

kha   khi   khu   da   di   du   dha   dhi   dhu

رَ   رِ   رُ   زَ   زِ   زُ   سَ   سِ   سُ

ra   ri   ru   za   zi   zu   sa   si   su

| YouTube | Video: Reading: Level 1 Part A |

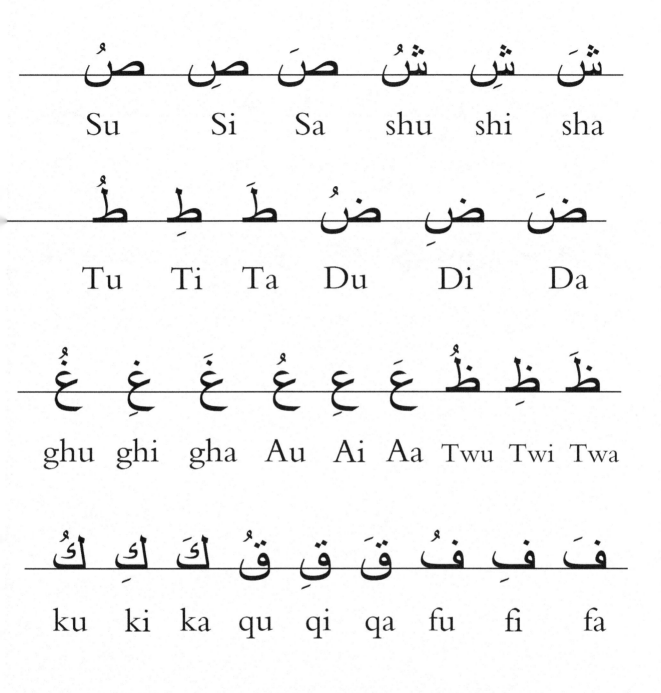

شَ شِ صَ صِ صُ شُ شِ شَ

Su   Si   Sa   shu   shi   sha

طُ طَ طِ ضُ ضَ ضِ

Tu   Ti   Ta   Du   Di   Da

غُ غِ غَ عُ عِ عَ ظُ ظِ ظَ

ghu   ghi   gha   Au   Ai   Aa   Twu   Twi   Twa

كُ كِ كَ قُ قِ قَ فُ فِ فَ

ku   ki   ka   qu   qi   qa   fu   fi   fa

You Tube	Video: Reading: Level 1 Part A
	Video: Reading: Level 1 Part B

نُ نِ نَ مُ مِ مَ لُ لِ لَ

nu ni na mu mi ma lu li la

ءُ ءِ ءَ يُ يِ يَ وُ وِ وَ هُ هِ هَ

'u 'i 'a yu yi ya wu wi wa hu hi ha

YouTube Video: Reading: Level 1 Part C

Exercise

Colour the leave with the colour of the same same sound below.

a = yellow   ba = green   ta = pink   tha = grey
i = red   bi = orange   ti = brown   thi = golden
u = blue   bu = purple   tu = black   thu = white

Write the number of the sound on the cup of the Arabic letter.

ja = 1   Ha = 4   kha = 7   da = 10
ji = 2   Hi = 5   khi = 8   di = 11
ju = 3   Hu = 6   khu = 9   du = 12

Help each car find the right house with the same sound.

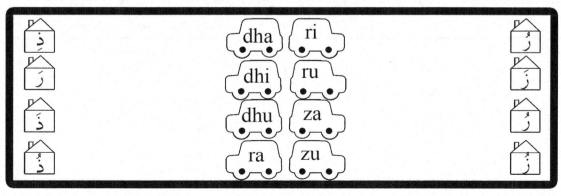

116

Exercise

Colour the pictuire according to the sounds below.

sa = Brown   sha = purple   Sa = yellow

si = Green   shi = orange   Si = light blue

su = red   shu = pink   Su = light blue

Exercise

Help each fisherman to catch the right fish with the same sound.

Exercise

Help each captain find his ship with the same sound and colour it.

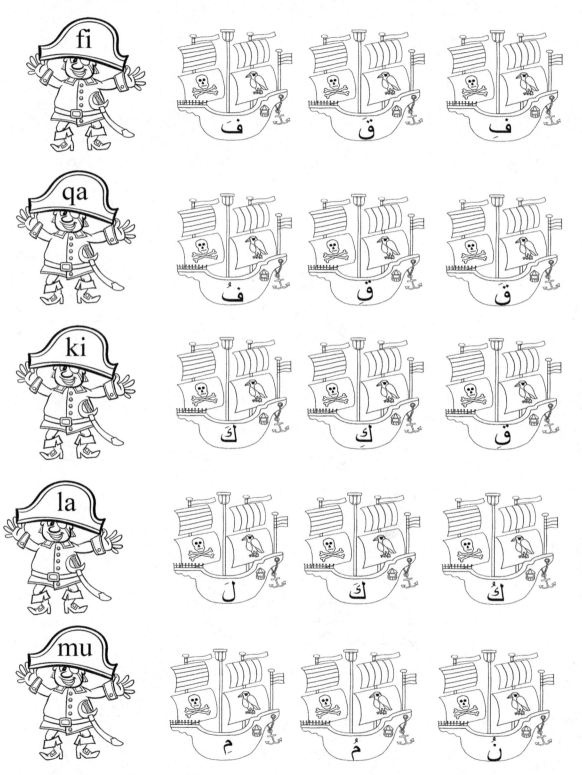

Exercise

Write the number of they on the treasure chest which match the sound.

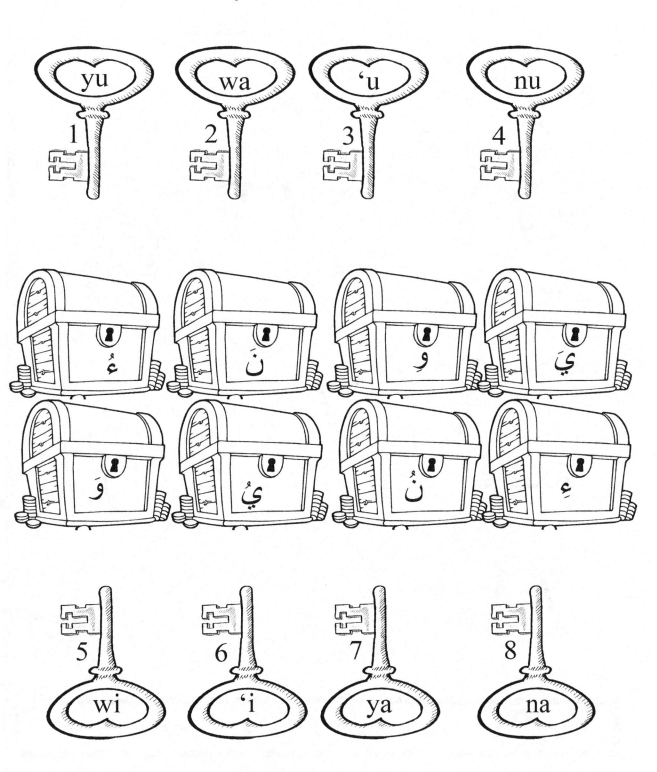

Section B: Conversation
Emotions

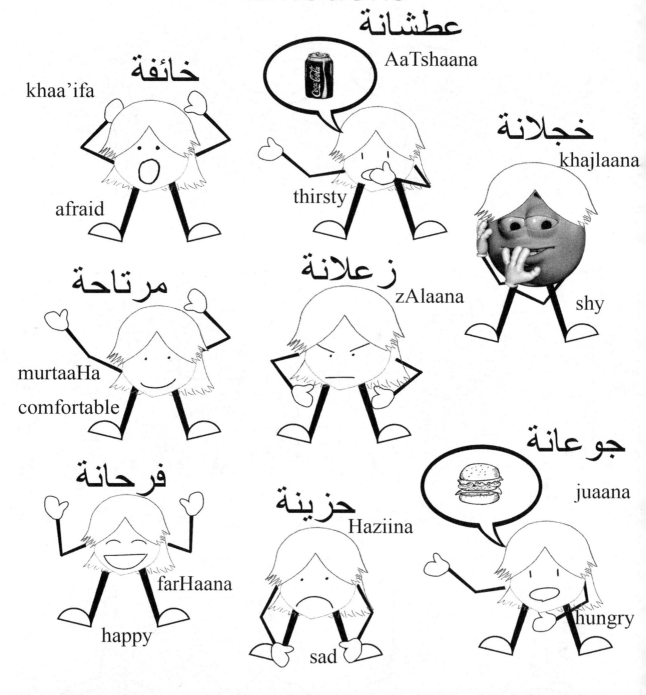

عطشانة
AaTshaana
thirsty

خائفة
khaa'ifa
afraid

خجلانة
khajlaana
shy

مرتاحة
murtaaHa
comfortable

زعلانة
zAlaana

فرحانة
farHaana
happy

حزينة
Haziina
sad

جوعانة
juaana
hungry

You Tube Video: Lesson 7: Part 2: Emotions : She

Exersize

Tick ✓ the correct box.

عطشانة
AaTshaana

حزينة
Haziina

خائفة
khaa'ifa

زعلانة
zAlaana

فرحانة
farHaana

122

Exersize

Tick  the correct box.

Writing Practise

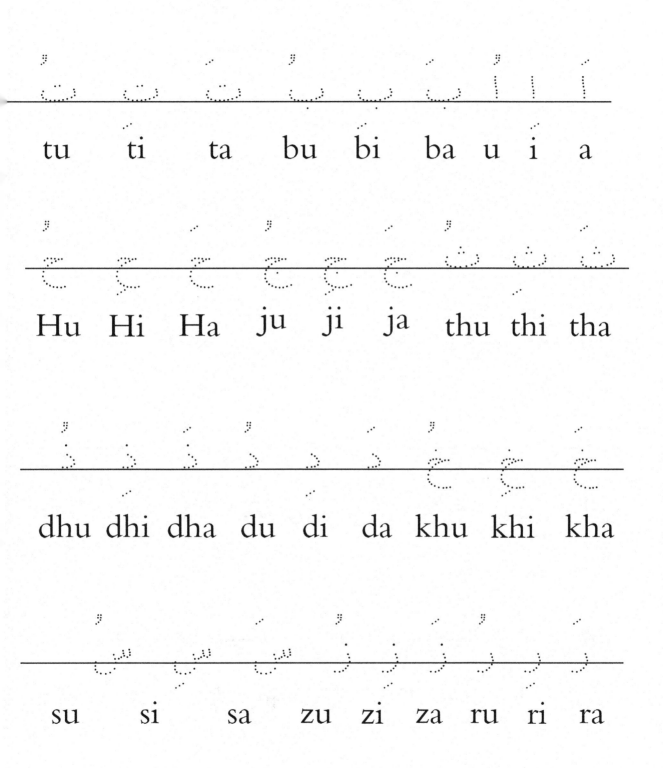

tu   ti   ta   bu   bi   ba   u   i   a

Hu   Hi   Ha   ju   ji   ja   thu   thi   tha

dhu   dhi   dha   du   di   da   khu   khi   kha

su   si   sa   zu   zi   za   ru   ri   ra

Writing Practise

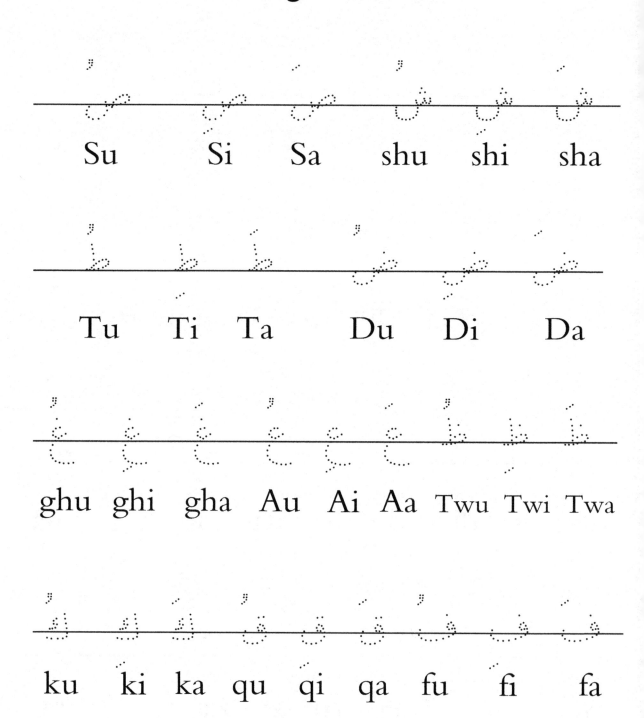

Su   Si   Sa   shu   shi   sha

Tu   Ti   Ta   Du   Di   Da

ghu ghi gha Au Ai Aa Twu Twi Twa

ku   ki   ka   qu   qi   qa   fu   fi   fa

Writing Practise

nu ni na mu mi ma lu li la

'u 'i 'a yu yi ya wu wi wa hu hi ha

نُ nu

Vocabulary

English	Transliteration	Arabic
afraid	khaa'ifa	خائفة
hungry	juAaana	جوعانة
thirsty	AaTshaana	عطشانة
sad	Haziina	حزينة
angry	zAlaana	زعلانة
comfortable	murtaaHa	مرتاحة
shy	khashlaana	خجلانة
happy	farHaana	فرحانة

Assessment : Emotions

Listen to your teacher and mark the picture with a X which he/she says.

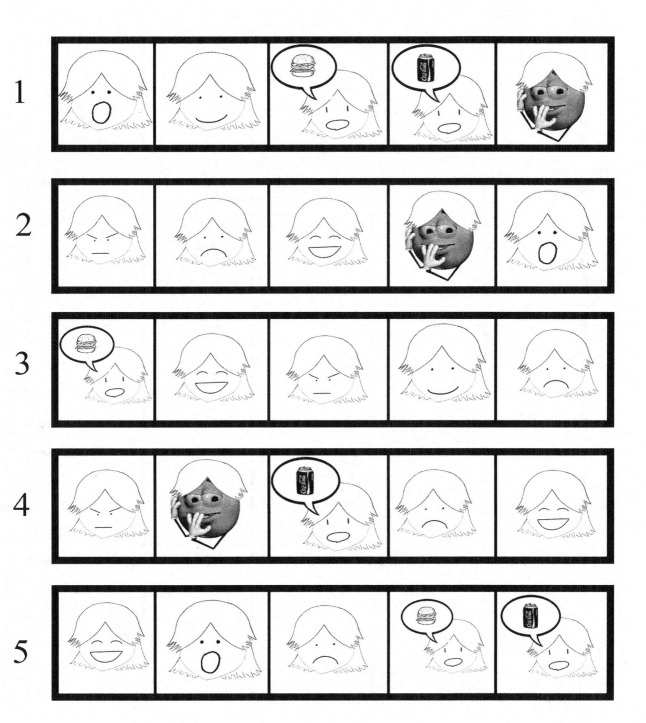

Assessment : Emotions

Listen to your teacher and mark the picture with a X which he/she says.

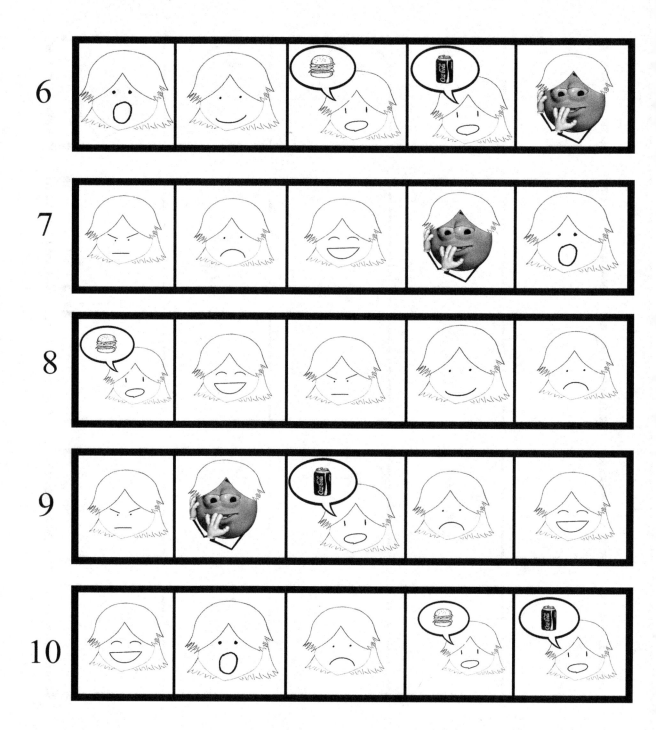

CPSIA information can be obtained
at www.ICGtesting.com
Printed in the USA
FSOW04n2006150716
22819FS